Middle Eastern
BIBLE

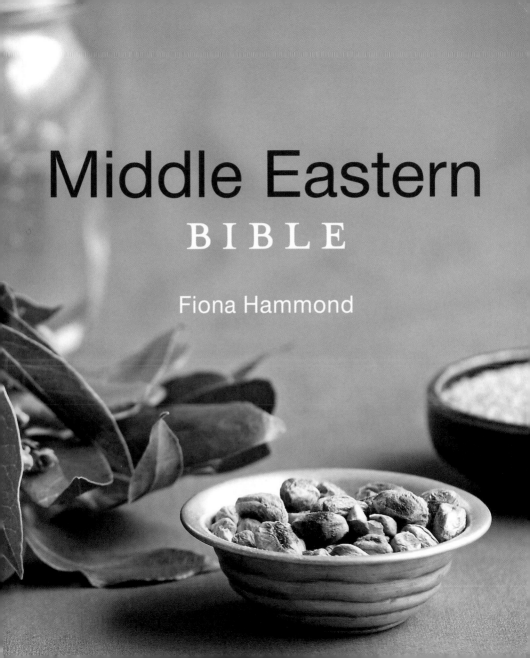

Middle Eastern

BIBLE

Fiona Hammond

Contents

Introduction

Middle Eastern cooking is as complex and varied as the ancient and diverse region from which it comes. In this book you'll find recipes from Turkey, Syria, Lebanon, Jordan, Iraq, Saudi Arabia and Iran (formerly Persia). Egypt is also included, for while it is geographically part of North Africa its cuisine arguably relates more closely to that of the Middle East.

The food of the Middle East, perhaps more than any other of the world's regions, continues to reflect the dietary and culinary traditions of the past. Rice and grains, meat and poultry, vegetables, fruits, yoghurt, oil and herbs were the staples of the poor; while the legacy of the Persian and Ottoman empires included extravagant dishes characterised by heady fragrances, exotic spices, sweet–sour flavours and decorative garnishes.

Middle Eastern Basics

The Middle East has no exact boundaries, its borders having been shuffled regularly over thousands of years, through conflict and invasion, migration and colonisation. But it is generally said to encompass the countries that surround the Persian Gulf, from Iran and the Arabian peninsula in southwest Asia to Turkey. Northeast Africa is sometimes included. 'The Fertile Crescent', which includes modern-day Iraq, Syria, Lebanon, Israel, Kuwait, Jordan, south-eastern Turkey and west and south-western Iran, was where one of the world's earliest civilisations, Mesopotamia, and its three largest religions – Islam, Judaism and Christianity – were founded.

Through the centuries the region's diverse cultures and traditions intermingled and inevitably influenced each other. Being at the junction of Asia and Europe, the area also benefited from the development of the spice trade, acquiring new ingredients and flavours. Its varied landscapes, from desert to bountiful coasts, yielded a vast range of produce.

Regional Ingredients & Flavours

The cuisine of the Middle East has myriad subtle variations, but can be roughly grouped according to four broad geographical regions. Ingredients such as yoghurt, olives and olive oil, rice and grains, nuts and seeds, fruits, herbs and spices are universal staples.

The food of **Turkey** reflects not only its position nestled between Asia and eastern Europe but also several hundred years of Ottoman rule. The Ottoman rulers were reputed for their kitchen skills and extravagance. Lamb is the chief meat, with cooking methods ranging from grilling to slow-roasting; kebabs are a Turkish invention. Yoghurt is used to flavour dishes from soups to cakes, to tenderise meat, and enjoyed as a side dish. Favoured herbs include dill, mint, parsley and bay; allspice, cinnamon and paprika are widely used spices. Coffee drinking is a favourite pastime, as it is throughout the Middle East.

Syria, Lebanon and Jordan, at the heart of the Fertile Crescent, enjoy a wide variety of produce from their prolific soils. Syria and Lebanon, bordering the eastern Mediterranean, enjoyed the bounty of the spice route between Asia and Europe: rosewater and orange-blossom water perfume syrups and pastries; aromatic mixtures such as za'atar add flavour to many dishes.

Iranian food is perhaps the most refined of the Middle Eastern cuisines. The ancient Persian Empire was a time of opulent banquets and today lavish rice dishes often take precedence at the table, accompanied with the substantial stew-like sauces known as khoreshtha, made with meat or poultry, vegetables, fruits, herbs and spices. Fruits such as pomegranates, sour cherries and quinces are used in both savoury and sweet dishes.

Egypt encompasses both vast desert lands as well as the lush valley of the Nile river. As in ancient times, agriculture provides staple ingredients such as grains (especially wheat and barley), vegetables (including a native bean called ful), fruit and nuts, poultry and lamb.

Techniques & Equipment

Middle Eastern cooking techniques are generally simple and the ingredients not hard to find. A few dishes need time for marinating or slow cooking, but this is fundamental in a culture where taking time to prepare and share good food is at the heart of life.

Many foods are grilled – this is done directly over hot coals or over flameless wood embers. A hibachi is excellent for this method of cooking. If using metal skewers, choose the square-edged type, as they hold the ingredients more successfully and will not roll around on the grill. Bamboo skewers should be soaked in water for at least 20 minutes before threading, to prevent them burning.

A mortar and pestle for grinding spices and other flavourings are highly recommended. A blender or food processor will make light work of any mixing. Otherwise your existing utensils – including saucepans (preferably heavy-based), one or more frying pans and a good-quality casserole pot – will be enough.

Essential Ingredients

OIL & BUTTER

Olive oil and clarified butter are preferred for cooking throughout the Middle East. If standard butter is used, it is usually the unsalted variety. Olive oil does not coagulate when cool and is essential to use for the many dishes that are eaten cold. The clarified butter known as samneh in the Middle East is used widely for its rich distinctive flavour and its ability to reach high temperatures without burning. Ghee can be used instead.

To make **samneh** at home, melt unsalted butter in a saucepan over low heat until it bubbles. Skim off any rising froth, then pour the remaining clear yellow liquid (leaving the solid milk residue in the pan) through a muslin-lined sieve into a jar. Seal the jar and store in the refrigerator for up to 6 months. Because of the excellent keeping qualities of clarified butter, it is a good idea to make a large amount in one go.

YOGHURT

A creamy, Greek-style yoghurt is best.

For many recipes **drained yoghurt** is specified. To make about 1½ cups, you will need 2 cups (500 ml/17fl oz) full-fat yoghurt. Line a non-metal sieve with a large piece of muslin (or a new loose-weave kitchen wipe) folded in half and place over a bowl or jug. Fold over the corners of the cloth to cover the yoghurt, then refrigerate and allow to drain for 2–4 hours until the yoghurt is the consistency of double cream.

Goat's milk yoghurt, which does not curdle when heated, was originally the chief type used. Today most yoghurt is made from cow's milk and requires stabilising to prevent it from curdling during lengthy cooking. To make 2 cups **stabilised yoghurt**, put 2 cups (500 ml/17 fl oz) Greek-style yoghurt in a heavy-based saucepan over low heat and stir until it thins a little. Mix 1 tablespoon cornflour and ½ teaspoon salt with 1 tablespoon water to form a paste, and stir into the yoghurt in one direction.

Bring to a gentle simmer, still stirring in one direction, until well combined, and cook for 5–10 minutes or until thickened.

HERBS & SPICES

Just about every Middle Eastern dish is touched by the fragrance and distinctive flavours of herbs or spices. Though every region or country has its own favoured varieties, each household or restaurant kitchen is likely to make its own blends. In the same way, you can adjust the recipes in this book to suit your personal preference.

The most common **herbs** used in Middle Eastern dishes are thyme, bay, mint, oregano and parsley. If buying dried herbs, choose a reputable food store with a high turnover to avoid musty produce. Otherwise use fresh leaves from your garden or buy fresh bunches from your greengrocer. Growing herbs at home is easy and ensures a satisfying supply for most of the year. If you do grow your own, the flavour is at its best when the plant is flowering and growth is at its peak.

This is also the perfect time to pick any surplus crop and dry the leaves for later use. To **dry your own herbs**, hang bunches of thyme and bay in an airy place to dry, then store in a sealed container in a cool dark place for up to 3 months. To dry mint and oregano, spread over wire racks in an airy place out of direct sunlight, then store as above. Bear in mind that drying times can vary: soft-leaf herbs can take 1 week, while the stalks of thyme and the bay leaf take up to 2 weeks.

For the best flavour, buy **spices** in small quantities and store them in airtight containers in a cool dark place for no longer than 3 months. Toasting and grinding whole spices, rather than buying them already ground, gives the best results in terms of both freshness and fragrance. To do this, place individual spices in a heavy-based frying pan over medium heat and toast, stirring occasionally, until the spices are aromatic and have darkened a little (1–2 minutes): be careful not to let the spices burn, as they will become bitter. Once toasted, grind the spices in a mortar or use a small (spice or coffee) grinder reserved for the purpose.

NUTS & SEEDS

Middle Eastern cooks use lots of them: almonds, hazelnuts, pine nuts, pistachios, walnuts, sesame seeds. Buy in small quantities and store in a sealed container in the refrigerator to keep them fresher longer.

For savoury dishes, nuts are generally shallow-fried or toasted before adding. To fry, heat about 1 cm (⅜ in) olive oil in a frying pan and fry nuts in small batches for 2–3 minutes, watching carefully, until golden. Drain well on paper towels. To toast, place nuts in a 180°C (360°F) oven for 10–15 minutes until golden brown: watch carefully that they do not burn.

RICE

Long-grain is the rice of choice for dishes where fluffy, separate grains are preferred. Fragrant Iranian rice is available from some Middle Eastern food stores, but basmati rice is a popular alternative. Short-grain rice, which is starchier and becomes sticky when cooked, is mostly used for puddings and stuffings.

Long-grain rice is typically **washed** before use to remove excess starch. Place the measured rice in a bowl, pour enough boiling water over to cover and stir several times. Drain, then rinse under running water until water runs clear. Drain well again and use as required.

To make 4–6 serves (about 3½ cups) **plain rice**, wash 2 cups (400 g/28 oz) long-grain rice as described above. Heat 2 tablespoons samneh or olive oil in a heavy-based saucepan over medium heat. Stir in rice until well coated and cook for 2 minutes until rice is translucent. Increase heat to high, add 3 cups (750 ml/25 fl oz) water and bring to the boil. Cover pan, reduce heat to low and cook for 20 minutes. Turn off heat and leave for 10 minutes before removing lid. Fluff the rice with a fork to serve.

Mezes

Mezes (or mezzes) are integral to Middle Eastern life and are a great example of the people's generosity and hospitality. These small treats are to be enjoyed at leisure – taking time to relax and catch up with life.

A meze can be as simple or elaborate as the cook chooses: it is often a small version of a main dish, such as mini kebabs, little kibbeh or small pastries. The choice is endless. When time is on your side, platters of felafel, stuffed vegetables and filled vine leaves make great party food. For quick or impromptu mezes, offer olives, dips and pickles accompanied with warmed flatbread for gathering up the delicious morsels.

< Cheese & Herb Pastry Triangles (page 16)

Cheese & Herb Pastry Triangles

Makes 24

8 sheets filo pastry

150 g (5 oz) butter or samneh, melted

CHEESE FILLING

180 g (6½ oz) fetta cheese

180 g (6½ oz) haloumi cheese, drained and grated

2 tablespoons finely chopped fresh dill

2 tablespoons finely chopped fresh mint

2 tablespoons finely chopped fresh parley

2 tablespoons finely chopped spring onions (white part only)

¼ teaspoon freshly grated nutmeg

⅓ cup toasted pine nuts

freshly ground black pepper

For the filling, mash together the fetta and haloumi, using the back of a fork. Stir in the herbs, nutmeg, pine nuts and pepper. Set aside.

Preheat the oven to 190°C (375°F). Line two oven trays with baking paper.

Cut the filo sheets lengthways into three. (Cover the unfilled sheets with a lightly dampened tea towel while you are working, to prevent the pastry drying out.) Take one strip at a time and brush lightly with samneh or butter. Place a heaped teaspoonful of the cheese mixture near one end of the strip, towards one side, then fold one corner over the filling, on the diagonal, to form a triangle.

Fold the filled triangle over to the other side, keeping its shape, and then continue to fold in this way to the end of the filo strip (make sure there are no holes for the filling to escape through). Brush surface with butter, then place triangle on baking tray. Repeat with remaining pastry and filling.

Bake triangles in preheated oven for 12–15 minutes or until golden-brown. Serve hot or at room temperature.

๑ These pastries can be prepared in advance and frozen (unbaked). Defrost before baking.

Eggplant Dip

Babaganouj

Makes about 1½ cups

2 medium-sized firm eggplants
(about 450 g/1 lb in total)

3 tablespoons (60 ml/2 fl oz)
freshly squeezed lemon juice

⅓ cup (80 ml/3 fl oz) tahini

2 cloves garlic, crushed with
1 teaspoon salt

1 teaspoon ground cumin
(optional)

1 teaspoon chopped flat-leaf
parsley, for garnish

warmed flatbread or raw
vegetable sticks, to serve

Place eggplants over a charcoal grill or directly over a gas flame. Turn the eggplants occasionally, cooking until skin is blackened all over and the flesh is tender. Transfer to a bowl and set aside until cool enough to handle. Peel away charred skin and discard.

Place the eggplant flesh in the bowl of a food processor with the lemon juice, tahini, garlic and cumin. Blend until well combined. Taste, and add extra tahini, lemon juice or garlic, if needed. It should have a wonderful smoky flavour.

Spread in a shallow bowl, and serve sprinkled with chopped parsley.

ᔕ Babaganouj will keep for up to 4 days in an airtight container in the refrigerator.

Fried Cheese

Serves 4–6

**250 g (9 oz) hard white salty
cheese (haloumi, kasseri or
kefalograviera)**

olive oil for frying

**1 lemon, cut into wedges,
to serve**

Pat cheese dry with paper towel. Cut into 2-cm (¾-in) cubes.

Pour oil into a frying pan to a depth of about 1 cm (⅜ in) and place over medium–high heat. Put in the cheese cubes and cook, turning, until lightly golden on all sides (about 2 minutes in total). Drain on paper towels.

Serve immediately, with lemon wedges for squeezing. Spiced green olives (page 36) make a good accompaniment.

Spiced Chickpea Croquettes

Felafel

Makes about 30

2 cups dried chickpeas

1 onion, finely chopped

2 cups chopped fresh parsley

2 cups chopped fresh coriander

3 cloves garlic, crushed with
  2 teaspoons salt

1 teaspoon ground coriander

1 teaspoon ground cumin

sunflower oil for deep-frying

tahini sauce (see note page 31),
  to serve

Place chickpeas in a large bowl, cover with water and soak overnight. Drain well. Place in a food processor with the onion and blend until mixture forms a paste. Add herbs, garlic and spices, and blend until ingredients are well combined. (Depending on size of processor, you may have to do this in two batches.) Set aside for 30 minutes.

Using wet hands, shape the mixture into walnut-sized balls or egg-shapes. Place on a tray. (They can be prepared up to this stage a day ahead, covered with cling wrap and refrigerated.)

In a deep pan or a wok, heat oil to 190°C (375°F). Deep-fry the felafel, about five at a time, for 3–5 minutes, turning, until they are a rich dark-brown. Drain on paper towels and keep warm while you fry the remainder.

Serve hot with tahini sauce alongside. Also delicious accompanied with tomato and cucumber salad with sumac (page 71).

Dukkah

Makes about ½ cup

⅓ cup coriander seeds

¼ cup cumin seeds

⅔ cup sesame seeds

¼ cup hazelnuts

½ teaspoon sea salt

¼ teaspoon freshly ground
black pepper

Preheat the oven to 150°C (300°F).

Prepare all the ingredients separately. Place coriander seeds in a small dry frying pan over medium heat and toast for about 2 minutes, until aromatic, shaking the pan from time to time. Transfer to a mortar and pound until finely crushed (don't over-work to a paste). Repeat this process with the cumin and sesame seeds.

Place the hazelnuts on a baking tray and toast in preheated oven for 10 minutes or until golden. When cool enough to handle, place in a clean tea towel and rub off skins. Crush the nuts in a mortar or food processor, being careful not to over-work and turn it into a paste.

Combine the hazelnuts with the ground spices and seeds, then stir the salt and pepper through.

Serve with extra-virgin olive oil and bread for dunking.

- Dukkah will keep for 2 months in an airtight container in a dark place, though for maximum flavour it's best used within a few weeks.
- This mixture is sometimes used as a crust for meat or fish, or to add crunch to vegetable dishes.

Herbed Labne Balls

Makes about 50

1 cup finely chopped fresh
    flat-leaf parsley

1 cup finely chopped fresh dill

2 quantities labne balls (see
    note page 238)

flatbread or Turkish bread,
    to serve

Place the herbs in separate bowls. Remove the labne balls from the oil and roll in the herbs to coat evenly – roll half the balls in the parsley and half in the dill.

Serve at room temperature with warmed flatbread or slices of char-grilled Turkish bread.

Chickpea Dip

Hummus

Makes about 3 cups

1 cup dried chickpeas

⅓ cup (80 ml/3 fl oz) tahini

½ cup (125 ml/4 fl oz) freshly squeezed lemon juice

3 tablespoons (60 ml/2 fl oz) olive oil, plus extra for drizzling

2 cloves garlic, chopped

1 teaspoon ground cumin

salt

ground sweet paprika, for garnish

Place chickpeas in a large bowl (they will double in volume when soaked), cover with water and soak overnight.

Drain the chickpeas and place in a large saucepan with enough water to cover them by 5 cm (2 in). Bring to the boil over high heat, then reduce to a simmer and cook for an hour or until chickpeas are very tender. Drain, reserving 1 tablespoon of whole chickpeas and ¼ cup of the cooking liquid.

Place chickpeas, reserved cooking water, tahini, lemon juice, oil, garlic and cumin in a food processor, and blend until smooth. Season with salt, and adjust flavour to taste with additional lemon juice or tahini. Add some water if you prefer a thinner consistency.

Spoon hummus into a shallow bowl. Scatter with the reserved chickpeas, then drizzle with extra oil and sprinkle with paprika. Serve warm or at room temperature.

🐎 You can use drained, canned chickpeas (2 × 400-g/14-oz cans) instead of dried ones.

🐎 Hummus can be stored in an airtight container in the refrigerator for up to 3 days. Bring to room temperature before serving.

Fenugreek Dip

Makes about 1 cup

3 tablespoons fenugreek seeds

2 spring onions, finely chopped

2 fresh green chillies, deseeded and finely chopped

2 cloves garlic, chopped

1 teaspoon baharat (page 237)

1 cup chopped fresh coriander

2 tomatoes, peeled and chopped

2½ tablespoons (50 ml/1¾ fl oz) freshly squeezed lemon juice, or to taste

flatbread, to serve

Place fenugreek seeds in 1 cup water and leave to soak overnight (this removes any bitterness). Drain well.

Place the fenugreek seeds in a blender or food processor with the remaining ingredients (except the bread). Blend to a coarse paste. Taste, and add more lemon juice if needed.

Serve with flatbread.

Spiced Fetta & Yoghurt

Serves 6–8

1½ cups drained yoghurt (see page 9)

250 g (9 oz) fetta cheese, crumbled

1 clove garlic, crushed with ¼ teaspoon sea salt

½ teaspoon ground paprika

¼ teaspoon dried chilli flakes (optional)

1 teaspoon fresh thyme leaves, or ½ teaspoon dried mint

2 tablespoons coarsely chopped kalamata olives

1 tablespoon (20 ml/¾ fl oz) extra-virgin olive oil

flatbread, to serve

Place yoghurt and fetta in a bowl. Using the back of a fork, mash the fetta and mix it into the yoghurt. Stir in the garlic, paprika, chilli, thyme or mint, olives, and a grinding of black pepper. Mix well.

Serve in a shallow bowl, drizzled with the olive oil and accompanied with warmed flatbread.

Tahini Dip

Makes about 1 cup

½ cup (125 ml/4 fl oz) tahini

1 clove garlic, crushed

½ teaspoon ground cumin

3 tablespoons (60 ml/2 fl oz)
  freshly squeezed lemon juice

3 tablespoons (60 ml/2 fl oz)
  warm water

salt

Place tahini, garlic, cumin, half the lemon juice and half the water in the bowl of a food processor. Process until well combined, then blend in remaining lemon juice and enough water to produce the consistency you want. Season to taste with salt.

- To make tahini sauce, simply add more water.
- To make green tahini sauce, add ½ cup finely chopped fresh flat-leaf parsley when blending the mixture. This is a delicious accompaniment to fish, grilled meats or felafel.

Smoked Capsicum & Tomato Dip

Makes about 1 ½ cups

450 g (1 lb) firm ripe tomatoes

2 large red capsicums

2 cloves garlic, crushed with
1 teaspoon salt

¼ teaspoon dried mint

1 teaspoon fresh thyme leaves

½ teaspoon ground sweet
paprika

¼ teaspoon crushed dried chilli
(or 1 fresh bird's eye chilli,
deseeded and finely chopped)

2 tablespoons (40 ml/1 ½ fl oz)
extra-virgin olive oil

2 teaspoons pomegranate
molasses

freshly ground black pepper

2 tablespoons chopped flat-leaf
parsley, for garnish

flatbread, to serve

Preheat grill or oven to maximum temperature. Grill or roast the tomatoes, turning occasionally, for 5–10 minutes or until skins blacken and blister on all sides. When cool enough to handle, peel off skins, discard seeds and reserve flesh.

Repeat this process with the capsicums, but cook for 10–12 minutes and then place in a plastic bag until cool enough to handle. Remove skin and seeds, and place flesh and any juices in the bowl of a food processor.

To the processor, add the tomato flesh, garlic, mint, thyme, paprika, chilli, oil, pomegranate molasses and a grinding of black pepper. Pulse until the ingredients are coarsely chopped and well mixed.

Transfer to a serving dish and garnish with parsley. Serve the dip at room temperature, with flatbread. (It is also good served with grilled meat skewers.)

ℊ Keep in an airtight container in the refrigerator for up to 3 days.

Little Spinach Parcels

Makes about 18

400 g (14 oz) spinach leaves, stems removed

1 tablespoon (20 ml/¾ fl oz) olive oil

1 onion, finely chopped

2 tablespoons (40 ml/1½ fl oz) freshly squeezed lemon juice

1 teaspoon ground sumac

salt and ground black pepper

100 g (3½ oz) crumbled fetta or haloumi cheese (optional)

1 quantity wholemeal pita bread dough (see note page 92), after first proving

Preheat the oven to 200°C (390°F). Lightly oil or line two baking trays.

Chop the spinach leaves coarsely. Heat the oil in a frying pan over medium heat, add onion and cook for 5 minutes until softened. Stir in the spinach and lemon juice, and cook until the spinach wilts and the liquid has evaporated. Stir in the sumac, season with salt and pepper, and set aside to cool slightly. Stir in cheese (if using).

Take golfball-sized pieces of dough and roll out to 10-cm (4-in) rounds. Place a tablespoon of spinach mixture in the centre of each round, brush edges with water and bring up the sides at three points over the filling, to form a triangular parcel. Press edges to seal, and transfer to baking tray.

Bake parcels in preheated oven for 10–12 minutes, or until golden. Serve hot or at room temperature.

Spiced Green Olives

Makes about 1 cup

1 cup green olives

1 teaspoon coriander seeds

1 clove garlic, sliced

3 tablespoons (60 ml/2 fl oz) olive oil

juice of 1 lemon

Rinse olives, drain and dry with paper towels. Using a mallet or rolling pin, hit each olive to crack open the flesh, leaving the pip intact.

Place coriander seeds in a small saucepan over low–medium heat and dry-roast for 2–3 minutes until aromatic. Add garlic, olive oil and olives to warm through, then remove from heat and stir in lemon juice. Serve warm or at room temperature.

ℭ Bashing the olives bruises the flesh and releases the oils. If preferred, you could split the olives by pressing down with the flat of a knife.

Soups & Salads

Across the Middle East, soups (shorbah, shourabat) are generally considered a main meal, whether for breakfast, lunch or dinner. There can be a fine line – a ladleful or two of liquid – between soups and stews. Soups are often filled with pulses, rice, vegetables and meat. Meat is often left on the bone, making for a richer-tasting dish and so allowing diners to identify the meat being used. Soup is always accompanied with bread.

Salads are part of every meal, be it a simple side dish of tomatoes, cucumbers and onion rings, or cold cooked vegetables. The popular salads tabbouleh and fattoush combine an earthiness of flavour with the freshness of abundant herbs – perfect for a light lunch. No matter how simple or involved the salad, care is always taken choosing fresh, quality ingredients that offer textural and colour contrasts.

< Iranian Beef & Herb Soup (page 40)

Iranian Beef & Herb Soup

Serves 4–6

2 tablespoons (40 ml/1½ fl oz) vegetable oil

2 large onions, finely sliced

400 g gravy beef (or other stewing beef), trimmed of fat and sinew, then cut into 1-cm (⅜-in) cubes

1½ cups cooked chickpeas

1 teaspoon baharat (page 237)

½ teaspoon ground turmeric

freshly ground black pepper

2 cups (500 ml/17 fl oz) beef stock

salt

1 cup lightly crushed dried vermicelli noodles

large handful fresh flat-leaf parsley, finely chopped

large handful fresh coriander, finely chopped

large handful fresh dill, finely chopped

1 cup (250 ml/8½ fl oz) Greek-style yoghurt

2 teaspoons dried mint, for garnish

Heat oil in a large, heavy-based saucepan over medium heat. Add onions and fry for 8–10 minutes or until golden. Remove half of the onions and set aside in a small bowl.

Add meat to the pan in batches and cook for 3 minutes to seal. Return all the meat to the pan and stir in the chickpeas, baharat and turmeric. Season with pepper.

Add the stock and 750 ml (25 fl oz) water to the pan and bring to the boil. Reduce heat to low–medium and simmer for 30–40 minutes or until meat is tender.

Increase heat to a rolling simmer. Season soup with salt, add the noodles and herbs, and cook for 5 minutes or until noodles are tender. (Add boiling water to thin the soup if necessary.)

Divide soup between bowls. Place a dollop of yoghurt on top and scatter with the reserved onion. Rub the dried mint between your fingers and sprinkle it over the yoghurt. Serve immediately.

Chicken Soup with Lemon & Rice

Serves 6–8

1 × 1-kg (2 lb 3-oz) chicken

2 sticks celery, chopped

1 carrot, chopped

2 cloves garlic, sliced

1 leek (white part only), sliced

2 bay leaves

1 cinnamon stick

6 white peppercorns

½ lemon

2 zucchini, diced or coarsely grated

1 cup cooked long-grain rice

2 tablespoons chopped fresh flat-leaf parsley

1 clove garlic, crushed with ½ teaspoon sea salt

about 3 tablespoons (60 ml/ 2 fl oz) freshly squeezed lemon juice

salt and ground white pepper

Place chicken, celery, carrot, garlic, leek, bay leaves, cinnamon, pepper-corns and lemon into a large stock pot. Add enough water to generously cover all the ingredients, bring to the boil over a high heat and then reduce to a gentle simmer. Cook for an hour, or until meat is falling off the bone (skim off any scum that appears on the surface during this time).

Lift out the chicken and set aside until cool enough to handle. Discard the bones and skin, and shred the meat. >

Strain stock through a fine sieve into a large clean saucepan and bring to a simmer. Add the zucchini and cook for 10 minutes. Return the chicken meat to the stock and stir in the rice, parsley and garlic. Add lemon juice to taste, and season if necessary with salt and pepper. Cook for 2 minutes, or until heated through. Serve immediately so that the rice does not overcook.

හ This soup can easily be adapted to make use of whichever vegetables are in season.

Silverbeet & Lentil Soup

Serves 4

3 tablespoons (60 ml/2 fl oz) olive oil

1 large onion, finely chopped

2 cloves garlic, finely sliced

1 cup dried brown lentils

1.5 L (3 pt 3 fl oz) chicken stock or water

1 large bunch silverbeet (or spinach), stems removed

½ cup fresh coriander leaves

3 tablespoons (60 ml/2 fl oz) freshly squeezed lemon juice

salt and freshly ground black pepper

lemon wedges, to serve

Heat oil in a large saucepan over medium heat and sauté onion for 5 minutes until softened. Add garlic and cook for 1 minute. Stir in the lentils, then add the stock and increase heat to high. Bring to the boil, then reduce heat and simmer for 45 minutes, or until lentils are soft.

Meanwhile, rinse silverbeet leaves well and chop roughly. Stir the silverbeet, coriander and lemon juice into the lentils, then season with salt and pepper. Cook for 5 minutes, until the silverbeet wilts. If the soup is too thick, add extra water.

Serve immediately with lemon wedges on the side.

&) You can prepare this soup a day ahead: cover and refrigerate until required, then reheat.

Minty Split-pea & Potato Soup

Serves 6

1½ cups dried green split peas

3 tablespoons (60 ml/2 fl oz) olive oil

1 onion, finely diced

1 teaspoon dried mint

1.5 L (3 pt 3 fl oz) vegetable or chicken stock

2 medium-sized potatoes, peeled and diced

1 teaspoon salt

¼ teaspoon ground white pepper

½ cup chopped fresh mint

extra-virgin olive oil, for drizzling

1 lemon, cut into 6 wedges

black olives, to serve

Remove any discoloured split peas, then rinse and drain well.

Heat the oil in a saucepan over medium heat. Add the onion and cook for 5 minutes until softened. Add the drained peas and dried mint, and stir for 30 seconds. Pour in the stock, bring to the boil (skim any rising scum from the surface), reduce heat and simmer, covered, for 30 minutes. Add the potatoes, salt and pepper, and continue to simmer for 20 minutes or until peas and potatoes are very tender. Stir in the fresh mint and cook for 1 minute, then adjust seasoning if needed.

Using a stick blender or food processor, purée soup in batches. Serve hot, drizzled with a little extra-virgin olive oil and accompanied with lemon wedges and olives.

Spiced Pumpkin & Tomato Soup

Serves 6

a 1.5-kg (3 lb 5-oz) butternut pumpkin, cut in half lengthways

2 tablespoons (40 ml/1½ fl oz) olive oil

1 onion, chopped

1 teaspoon ground paprika

1 teaspoon ground cumin

½ teaspoon ground turmeric

1 teaspoon ground coriander

1 teaspoon salt

freshly ground black pepper

800 g (1 lb 12 oz) canned chopped tomatoes

1 L (34 fl oz) chicken stock

1 cup (250 ml/8½ fl oz) drained yoghurt (see page 9)

3 tablespoons chopped fresh coriander leaves

Preheat the oven to 190°C (375°F). Oil a roasting dish.

Place the pumpkin halves in the roasting dish. Bake for 45–50 minutes or until just tender. Remove from oven and use a spoon to remove the seeds. Scrape the flesh from the skin, discard the skin and set flesh aside.

Heat olive oil in a heavy-based saucepan over low–medium heat. Add onions and sauté for 10 minutes until softened. Stir in spices, salt and pepper, and cook for 1 minute. Add pumpkin and cook for 5 minutes. Add tomatoes and stock, bring to the boil, then simmer for 20 minutes. Purée the soup until smooth. Season to taste with salt and pepper. Ladle into bowls, top with a dollop of yoghurt and sprinkle with coriander.

Cold Yoghurt Soup

Serves 4–6

2 Lebanese cucumbers,
coarsely grated

½ teaspoon sea salt

3 cups (750 ml/25 fl oz)
Greek-style yoghurt

½ cup (125 ml/4½ oz) sour
cream

3 spring onions (white parts
only), finely chopped

1 teaspoon chopped fresh dill

1 tablespoon chopped fresh
mint

Place cucumber in a colander, sprinkle with the salt and set aside to drain.

In a large bowl whisk together the yoghurt, sour cream and about ⅓ cup water. Lightly rinse and drain the cucumber, then stir into the yoghurt mixture with the spring onions, dill and mint. Combine well, cover, and refrigerate for an hour before serving.

Serve chilled.

Chickpea & Potato Salad

Serves 6

500 g (1 lb 5 oz) waxy potatoes
(e.g. kipfler), cut into 5-mm
(¼-in) slices

⅓ cup (80 ml/3 fl oz) olive oil

1 red onion, finely sliced

1½ cups cooked chickpeas

2 cloves garlic, crushed

½ teaspoon ground allspice

450 g (1 lb) tomatoes, peeled
and chopped

1 tablespoon chopped fresh
mint

salt and freshly ground black
pepper

1 cup coarsely chopped fresh
flat-leaf parsley

sumac, for garnish

Place potatoes in a saucepan of cold salted water over high heat, bring to the boil, then reduce heat and simmer for 15–20 minutes until just tender when pierced with a knife. Drain well.

Heat the oil in a large saucepan over medium heat. Add the onion and sauté for 5 minutes until softened. Stir in the drained potatoes with the chickpeas, garlic, allspice and tomatoes, mixing well. Bring to a simmer and cook for 5 minutes. Stir in mint, season to taste with salt and pepper, remove from heat and cool to room temperature.

Before serving, gently stir parsley through and sprinkle with sumac.

ɔ This dish is good alongside grilled chicken, or served as a meze.

Mixed Salad with Herbs

Serves 4–6

3 tablespoons (60 ml/2 fl oz)
  extra-virgin olive oil

3 tablespoons (60 ml/2 fl oz)
  freshly squeezed lemon juice

1 clove garlic, crushed with
  ½ teaspoon sea salt

freshly ground black pepper

1 bunch baby radishes, leaves
  and roots removed, and flesh
  thinly sliced

2 baby cos lettuce, leaves
  roughly chopped

1 Lebanese cucumber, peeled
  and cut into 1-cm (⅜-in)
  cubes

1 cup roughly chopped fresh
  mint

1 cup roughly chopped fresh
  flat-leaf parsley

4 spring onions, thinly sliced

2 tablespoons chopped fresh
  dill

Whisk together the oil, lemon juice and garlic in a small bowl. Season to taste with ground pepper.

Place the radishes, lettuce, cucumber and herbs in a salad bowl and toss gently to mix. Pour the dressing over and toss again gently to combine. Serve immediately.

Citrus & Watercress Salad

Serves 6

1 orange

1 lime

1 ruby grapefruit

2 tablespoons (40 ml/1½ fl oz) freshly squeezed lemon juice

1 tablespoon (20 ml/¾ fl oz) orange-blossom water

3 tablespoons (60 ml/2 fl oz) extra-virgin olive oil

salt and freshly ground black pepper

1 cup watercress or rocket leaves

2 avocados, peeled and flesh cut into cubes

Use a sharp knife to cut away the peel of the citrus fruits, removing all traces of white pith. Cut each piece of fruit into thin slices, removing any pips, then set aside.

In a small bowl whisk together the lemon juice, orange-blossom water and oil. Season lightly with salt and pepper.

Arrange citrus slices on a platter and scatter with the watercress and avocado. Drizzle dressing over.

🔊 Can be served as a refreshing accompaniment for fish.

Broad-Bean, Capsicum & Burghul Salad with Pomegranate Dressing

Serves 6

2 cups shelled small broad beans

2 red capsicums

1 quantity burghul pilaf (page 81), made with water

1 cup walnuts, coarsely chopped

½ cup chopped fresh flat-leaf parsley

POMEGRANATE DRESSING

1 tablespoon (20 ml/¾ fl oz) pomegranate molasses

1 clove garlic, crushed with ¼ teaspoon salt

3 tablespoons (60 ml/2fl oz) freshly squeezed lemon juice

⅓ cup (80 ml/3fl oz) extra-virgin olive oil

freshly ground black pepper

Cook broad beans in boiling salted water for 2 minutes. Drain, then refresh under cold water to stop the cooking process. Drain well, then slip off the skins to reveal the bright-green seeds, and set these aside.

Preheat the oven or grill to very hot and roast or grill the capsicums for 10–12 minutes, turning from time to time, until skins blacken and blister. Place in a plastic bag and leave until cool enough to handle, then peel off the skins and discard seeds (reserve any juices for the dressing). Chop the flesh. >

Whisk all the dressing ingredients together in a small bowl. Place cooled pilaf in a large bowl, add broad beans, capsicum, walnuts and parsley, and toss gently to combine. Stir dressing through.

❧ Serve as a light lunch or as an accompaniment to lamb or chicken.

Baby Beetroot Salad

Serves 6

450 g (1 lb) baby beetroot,
  stems and roots trimmed

2 tablespoons (40 ml/1½ fl oz)
  freshly squeezed lemon juice

3 tablespoons (60 ml/2 fl oz)
  extra-virgin olive oil

1 clove garlic, crushed with
  ½ teaspoon salt

1 tablespoon finely chopped
  fresh mint, plus extra leaves
  for garnish

freshly ground black pepper

Place beetroot in a medium-sized saucepan and cover with water. Bring to the boil and cook for 10 minutes or until tender, then drain well. When cool enough to handle, peel away skins by rubbing with your fingertips (wear latex gloves, to avoid stained hands). Cut the beetroot in half if preferred.

In a large bowl whisk together the lemon juice, oil, garlic and mint, then season with pepper. Add the warm beetroot to the dressing and toss to coat well. Spoon onto a serving plate and garnish with mint leaves.

ॐ To make a yoghurt dressing instead, reduce the oil to 2 tablespoons (40 ml/1½ fl oz) and stir in 1 cup (250 ml/8½ fl oz) plain yoghurt.

ॐ For a richer flavour, roast rather than boil the beetroot: roast at 180°C (360°F) for about 45 minutes or until tender.

Fennel, Celery & Cauliflower Salad with Shanklish & Pine Nuts

Serves 6

½ head cauliflower, separated into florets

⅓ cup (80 ml/3 fl oz) extra-virgin olive oil

⅓ cup (80 ml/3 fl oz) freshly squeezed lemon juice

sea salt and freshly ground black pepper

1 medium-sized fennel bulb, thinly sliced or shaved

4 sticks celery, thinly sliced on the diagonal

2 tablespoons toasted pine nuts

60 g (2 oz) crumbled shanklish cheese

Cook cauliflower in a saucepan of boiling salted water for 3 minutes. Drain, refresh in a bowl of ice-cold water, then drain well again.

Whisk together the oil and lemon juice, and season with salt and pepper.

Place fennel, celery and blanched cauliflower in a large bowl. Pour the dressing over and toss to combine well.

To serve, sprinkle salad with pine nuts and crumbled cheese.

℘ Shanklish is a round Lebanese goat's cheese available at Middle Eastern grocers. If unavailable, substitute any goat's cheese or fetta.

Cucumber & Fetta Salad

Serves 6

3 tablespoons (60 ml/2 fl oz)
extra-virgin olive oil

3 tablespoons (60 ml/2 fl oz)
freshly squeezed lemon juice

freshly ground black pepper

220 g (8 oz) fetta cheese

2 Lebanese cucumbers, cut
into 1-cm (⅝-in) dice

1 red onion, finely diced

1 tablespoon chopped fresh
mint

1 tablespoon chopped fresh
parsley

1 tablespoon chopped fresh dill

In a medium-sized bowl whisk together the oil and lemon juice, then season with pepper. Add the fetta and use the back of a fork to mash and mix it into the dressing. Stir in the cucumbers, onion and herbs, coating well with the dressing, then set aside for 30 minutes to allow the flavours to develop.

Serve as an accompaniment for grilled meats, with warmed flatbread alongside.

Toasted Bread Salad

Fattoush

Serves 6

1 Lebanese flatbread

½ head iceberg lettuce, roughly chopped

2 Lebanese cucumbers, cut into cubes

3 firm ripe tomatoes, cut into cubes

4 spring onions, finely sliced

1 green capsicum, diced

½ cup chopped fresh mint

1 cup chopped fresh flat-leaf parsley

1 cup purslane or watercress leaves

⅓ cup (80 ml/3 fl oz) freshly squeezed lemon juice

⅓ cup (80 ml/3 fl oz) olive oil

1 teaspoon sumac

½ teaspoon salt

freshly ground black pepper

Preheat the oven to 180°C (360°C).

Cut the bread into 3-cm (1¼-in) squares. Spread on a baking tray and bake in preheated oven for 8–10 minutes or until golden-brown and crisp. Set aside to cool.

Put the vegetables and herbs in a large serving bowl and scatter the toasted bread over the top.

Put the lemon juice, oil, sumac, salt and pepper in a screw-top jar and shake well. Pour dressing over the salad and toss gently to combine. Serve immediately, while bread is still crispy.

Sweet & Sour Eggplant Salad

Serves 4

2 medium-sized eggplants,
  cut into 2-cm (¾-in) cubes

salt

olive oil for frying

1 red onion, chopped

3 firm ripe tomatoes, peeled
  and chopped

2 tablespoons raisins

1 tablespoon (20 ml/¾ fl oz)
  pomegranate molasses

2 tablespoons (40 ml/1½ fl oz)
  freshly squeezed lemon juice

1 tablespoon (20 ml/¾ fl oz)
  honey

3 tablespoons chopped fresh
  flat-leaf parsley

Place eggplant in a colander and sprinkle generously with salt. Leave for 30 minutes, then rinse and drain well. Pat dry with paper towels.

Brush a large non-stick frying pan with oil. Over medium–high heat, fry the eggplant, stirring occasionally, until golden-brown. Transfer to a bowl.

Return frying pan to a medium heat and add 1 tablespoon oil. Add onion and cook for 10 minutes until softened. Return eggplant to the pan, add tomatoes, raisins, 100 ml (3½ fl oz) water, pomegranate molasses, lemon juice and honey, and stir. Reduce heat to low and cook for 15–20 minutes until eggplant is very soft. Stir parsley through, then set aside to cool to room temperature.

Serve with meat or fish dishes, or with warmed flatbread as a snack.

Lentil Salad

Serves 4–6

1 cup Puy lentils

½ cup chopped fresh flat-leaf parsley

1 red onion, finely diced

2 firm ripe tomatoes, deseeded and flesh diced

⅓ cup chopped fresh coriander

sea salt and freshly ground black pepper

DRESSING

2½ tablespoons (50 ml/1¾ fl oz) walnut oil

2½ tablespoons (50 ml/1¾ fl oz) extra-virgin olive oil

3 tablespoons (60 ml/2 fl oz) freshly squeezed lemon juice, or to taste

½ teaspoon ground cumin

For the dressing, whisk all the ingredients together in a small bowl.

Place lentils in a small saucepan and cover with cold water. Bring to the boil, cover and reduce heat to low–medium. Simmer for 25–30 minutes or until lentils are tender. Drain well and return to the saucepan (off the heat). Stir in the dressing and parsley, then set aside to cool to room temperature.

When ready to serve, stir onion, tomatoes and coriander through the lentils. Season lightly with salt and pepper.

🐄 Dark-brown lentils are more common in kitchens of the Middle East. Puy lentils are suggested for this salad as they have a beautiful slate-green colouring, wonderful earthy flavour, and hold their shape well.

Spinach with Yoghurt

Borani esfanaj

Serves 6 as a side dish

450 g (1 lb) spinach leaves,
thick stems removed

2 tablespoons (40 ml/1½ fl oz)
olive oil

1 onion, finely sliced

1 cup (250 ml/8½ fl oz) drained
yoghurt (see page 9)

1 clove garlic, crushed with
½ teaspoon salt

freshly ground black pepper

2 tablespoons chopped walnuts
(optional)

Chop the spinach leaves coarsely.

Heat oil in a non-stick frying pan over medium heat. Add onion and sauté
for 5 minutes until softened. Add the spinach and cook for about 5 minutes
or until the leaves have wilted and all the liquid has evaporated. Set aside
to cool.

Combine yoghurt and garlic in a large bowl and season with pepper. Add
the spinach and toss well until leaves are coated with the yoghurt dressing.
Spoon salad onto a serving platter and scatter with walnuts if using.

ഔ This simple and refreshing salad is equally good as a meze served with
flatbread, as a side dish, or as a sauce for kebabs and rice.

Tabbouleh

Serves 6–8

½ cup fine burghul (cracked wheat)

4 cups finely chopped fresh flat-leaf parsley

¼ cup finely chopped fresh mint

½ cup finely sliced spring onions

5 firm ripe roma tomatoes, diced

⅓ cup (80 ml/3 fl oz) olive oil

⅓ cup (80 ml/3 fl oz) freshly squeezed lemon juice

salt and freshly ground black pepper, to taste

baby cos lettuce leaves, to serve

Place burghul in a sieve, rinse under cold water and then place in a bowl with 1 cup (250 ml/8½ fl oz) water. Leave for 10 minutes, until grains have swelled, then drain well. Tip burghul into a clean tea towel and twist to squeeze out as much water as possible.

Place burghul, parsley, mint, spring onions and tomatoes in a large bowl. Combine oil and lemon juice, and season with salt and pepper, then pour dressing over burghul mixture and toss to combine.

Serve the salad with cos lettuce leaves for scooping it up. Can be served as an accompaniment to meat dishes or as a meal on its own.

80 Adjust the ingredients to suit your personal taste: add diced cucumber, red onion, extra mint, or more burghul if you prefer a nutty flavour.

Tomato & Cucumber Salad with Sumac

Serves 6

3 large ripe tomatoes, sliced

2 Lebanese cucumbers, cubed

1 clove garlic, crushed with
½ teaspoon salt

½ cup (125 ml/4 fl oz) drained
yoghurt (see page 9)

1 tablespoon (20 ml/¾ fl oz)
extra-virgin olive oil

1 tablespoon sumac

2 tablespoons chopped fresh
mint

Place tomato, cucumber, garlic and yoghurt in a bowl and toss gently to combine. Spoon onto a serving plate, drizzle with olive oil and sprinkle with sumac and mint.

Rice & Other Grains

Rice is grown in several parts of the Middle East and rice-cooking is taken very seriously. Each region has its own method and special dishes, such as chelou in Iran, pilaf in Turkey, and Indian-influenced dishes in the gulf states. Long-grain is the rice of choice, yielding fluffy, separate grains when cooked. Short-grain rice is mostly used for dishes such as puddings where it helps bind the ingredients together.

Wheat was one of the earliest crops grown in 'the Fertile Crescent'. Burghul or cracked wheat (more correctly, crushed wheat) has a long storage life and was traditionally the grain of the peasants. Fine burghul is used in recipes requiring a short soaking time, such as salads; the coarser variety can be cooked for a longer time without becoming soggy and is favoured for baked casseroles.

< Warm Moghrabieh Salad (page 74)

Warm Moghrabieh Salad

Serves 6

1 cup moghrabieh (giant couscous)

3 tablespoons (60 ml/2 fl oz) extra-virgin olive oil

juice of 1 lemon

12 cherry tomatoes, halved

1 red onion, finely sliced

½ cup walnut halves

⅓ cup kalamata olives, pitted and halved

2 cups watercress or purslane leaves

sea salt and freshly ground black pepper

Cook moghrabieh in a saucepan of boiling salted water for 20–25 minutes until tender. Drain well.

Transfer moghrabieh to a large bowl. While stil warm, pour the oil and lemon juice over and toss to coat well. Add the tomatoes, onion, walnuts, olives and watercress, and toss gently to combine. Season with salt and pepper.

Serve warm with grilled seafood or chicken.

Iranian Steamed Rice with a Crusty Base

Chelou

Serves 4–6

2 tablespoons salt

**2 cups long-grain rice, washed
(see page 13)**

**60 g (2 oz) ghee or samneh,
melted**

Bring 2 L (4 pt 4 fl oz) water to the boil in a large saucepan. Add salt and sprinkle in the rice. Stir continuously over high heat until water returns to the boil and then continue to boil for 5 minutes. Drain immediately.

Put half the ghee or samneh in a saucepan. Spread the rice evenly over the base of the saucepan, pour in the remaining ghee, then stretch a clean tea towel across the rim of the saucepan and put on the lid to secure. Place saucepan over a low heat for 25–30 minutes until the rice is cooked through and the grains fluffy and separate. A crisp golden-brown layer of rice will have formed on the base of the saucepan – this is considered a delicacy in Iran.

Dip the base of the pan into cold water for a minute to loosen the rice. Spoon the fluffy rice onto a serving platter. Scrape the crusty rice from the bottom of the pan, breaking it into pieces. Arrange crusty rice around the fluffy rice on the platter.

Saffron Rice with Nuts

Serves 6–8

3 cups (750 ml/25 fl oz) hot
chicken stock

2 tablespoons (40 ml/1½ fl oz)
olive oil

1 onion, finely chopped

pinch of saffron threads

3¾ cups long-grain rice,
washed (see page 13)

1 cinnamon stick

½ cup toasted blanched
almonds

½ cup toasted pine nuts

½ cup toasted shelled
pistachios

Place the stock in a saucepan and bring to the boil.

Meanwhile, heat the oil in a large heavy-based saucepan over medium heat.
Add the onion and sauté for 5 minutes until softened. Stir in the saffron and
rice, and cook until the rice is translucent and coated in oil. Add the boiling
stock and cinnamon stick, and cover pan. Reduce heat and simmer gently
for 15 minutes or until the rice is tender and holes appear across its surface.
Remove from heat and set aside, covered, for 10 minutes.

Spoon the rice into a serving dish and scatter with the freshly toasted nuts.

ॐ This is a good dish to serve with roasted meats.

ॐ For a stronger yellow colour, use ½ teaspoon saffron threads (or for a
less expensive alternative, add ¼ teaspoon ground turmeric).

Eggplant Pilaf from Turkey

Serves 4–6

450 g (1 lb) eggplants, cut into 2-cm (¾-in) cubes

½ cup (125 ml/4 fl oz) oil

1 onion, thinly sliced

1 clove garlic, finely chopped

½ teaspoon ground allspice

¼ teaspoon ground cinnamon

1 teaspoon salt

2 cups long-grain rice, washed (see page 13)

3 cups (750 ml/25 fl oz) chicken stock or water

2 tablespoons chopped fresh flat-leaf parsley

yoghurt or yoghurt and garlic sauce (see note page 246), to serve

Place eggplant cubes in a colander, sprinkle with salt and set aside for 30 minutes. Rinse under cold water, drain and pat dry with paper towels.

Heat half the oil in a frying pan over medium–high heat and fry the eggplant for 5–8 minutes until golden and tender. Remove eggplant with a slotted spoon and drain on paper towels.

Heat the remaining oil in a heavy-based saucepan over medium heat. Add the onion and cook for 5 minutes until softened. Stir in the garlic, spices, salt and eggplant, and cook for 1 minute. Add the rice and stock and bring to the boil without stirring. Cover pan, reduce heat and simmer for 15 minutes, until rice is cooked and the surface has a pitted appearance. >

Remove lid, stretch a clean tea towel across the saucepan rim, then replace lid. Set aside for 10 minutes to allow the cloth to absorb the steam.

Gently stir parsley through the rice. Served hot or cold, with yoghurt or yoghurt and garlic sauce, this is a perfect accompaniment to lamb or fish.

– If desired, add 400 g (14 oz) chopped tomatoes with the cooked eggplant and use ½ cup (125 ml/4 fl oz) less stock.

Burghul Pilaf

2 tablespoons (40 ml/1½ fl oz)
 olive oil

2 onions, finely sliced

1½ teaspoons ground allspice

¼ teaspoon salt

freshly ground black pepper

2 tablespoons golden raisins

1½ cups coarse burghul
 (cracked wheat)

2 cups (500 ml/17 fl oz)
 chicken stock or water

2 tablespoons chopped fresh
 flat-leaf parsley

Heat the oil in a saucepan over medium heat. Add onions and sauté for
10 minutes or until golden-brown. Stir in the allspice, salt, pepper, raisins
and burghul until coated with the oil. Pour in the stock and bring to the boil.
Cover pan, reduce heat and simmer for 10 minutes or until the stock is all
absorbed. Remove from heat and set aside for 10 minutes.

Stir the parsley through the burghul, using a fork to break up any lumps.
Serve the pilaf warm.

જી Golden raisins are lighter in colour than regular raisins. They are
available from Middle Eastern grocers. You could use sunmuscat
raisins (readily available at supermarkets) instead.

Rice & Vermicelli

Serves 6

2 tablespoons (40 g/1½ oz)
  unsalted butter

1 cup lightly crushed dried
  vermicelli

1½ cup long-grain rice,
  washed (see page 13)

3 cups (750 ml/25 fl oz)
  chicken stock or water

1 teaspoon salt

yoghurt or spinach with
  yoghurt (page 69), to serve

Melt the butter in a heavy-based saucepan over medium heat. Add vermicelli, stir to coat with the butter and then cook for 5 minutes or until golden-brown. Add the rice and cook for 2 minutes or until translucent. Add the stock and salt and bring to the boil. Reduce heat to low, cover and simmer gently for 15 minutes until rice is cooked and the liquid absorbed.

Serve hot with plain yoghurt, or with the spinach with yoghurt.

Turkish Carrot Pilaf

Serves 4–6

3 tablespoons (60 g/2 oz) unsalted butter

2 cups coarsely grated carrot

1 teaspoon sugar

¼ teaspoon ground allspice

freshly ground black pepper

2 cups long-grain rice, washed (see page 13)

3½ cups (875 ml/29 ½ fl oz) chicken stock

½ teaspoon salt

¼ teaspoon ground paprika, for garnish

Heat butter in a heavy-based saucepan over medium heat. Add carrot, stir to coat with the butter and then cook for 10 minutes until softened, stirring constantly. Add sugar, spices, pepper and rice, and cook for 2 minutes or until rice is translucent.

Pour stock into the pan and season with salt. Increase heat, bring to the boil and cover pan. Reduce heat to low and simmer for 15–20 minutes until rice is cooked.

Stretch a clean tea towel over the rim of the pan and replace the lid. Set aside for 10 minutes to allow the cloth to absorb the steam. Gently fluff up the rice with a fork and serve sprinkled with paprika.

Burghul & Spinach

Serves 4

1 cup coarse burghul (cracked wheat)

3 tablespoons (60 ml/2 fl oz) olive oil

1 onion, finely chopped

450 g (1 lb) spinach leaves, roughly chopped

1 teaspoon ground allspice

½ teaspoon ground cumin

1 teaspoon salt

freshly ground black pepper

¼ cup raisins

300 ml (10 fl oz) vegetable or chicken stock

Place burghul in a sieve, rinse under cold running water and drain.

Heat the oil in a large saucepan over medium heat. Add the onion and cook for 5 minutes until softened, then stir in the drained burghul and all the remaining ingredients. Bring to a low simmer, cover, and cook for 10–15 minutes until all the liquid has been absorbed and the burghul is tender. (Add a little extra water if the burghul is too dry.)

Serve warm.

Bread & Pastries

Throughout the Middle East, bread, like rice, is eaten at every meal. It is made in various styles, both leavened and unleavened: the most popular is the Arabic flatbread known as pita (khoubiz). This soft chewy round, with its central air pocket, is the perfect vessel for fillings such as felafel, kebabs and salad. Like other flatbreads, it also makes a convenient replacement for cutlery, being used to scoop up dips and soak up cooking juices and sauces.

There are also innumerable pastries, both savoury and sweet. Pastry is generally thought to have originated in the Middle East as a paper-thin dough, the precursor of more modern European 'pastes'. Pastry dishes are made whenever there is a celebration. Many comprise layers of filo pastry interspersed with a filling. Savoury versions are aromatic with herbs and spices, while sweet ones are perfumed with the heady scents of honey and rosewater or orange-blossom water.

< Chicken & Spice Pilaf Pie (page 90)

Chicken & Spice Pilaf Pie

Yufkali pilaf

Serves 6–8

2 tablespoons (40 ml/1½ fl oz) olive oil

1 onion, finely chopped

1 large carrot, finely chopped

500 g skinless chicken thigh fillets, cut into 1-cm (⅜-in) cubes

½ cup sultanas or chopped dried apricots

½ teaspoon ground allspice

¼ teaspoon ground cinnamon

1 bay leaf

1 teaspoon salt

freshly ground black pepper

2½ cups (625 ml/21 fl oz) chicken stock or water

¾ cup long-grain rice

12 sheets filo pastry

125 g (4½ oz) unsalted butter, melted

½ cup slivered almonds, toasted

Heat oil in a large non-stick frying pan over medium heat. Add onion and cook for 5 minutes until softened, then add carrot and cook for a further 5 minutes. Increase heat to high, stir in chicken and cook for 2–3 minutes until meat whitens.

Add dried fruit, spices, bay leaf, salt and pepper to the pan, and mix well. Pour in the stock, reduce heat, cover and simmer for 10 minutes. Add remaining stock and bring to the boil. Stir in rice, return to the boil, then reduce heat, cover, and simmer gently for 20 minutes or until all the liquid is absorbed and the rice is just cooked. Remove from heat and set aside.

Meanwhile, preheat the oven to 180°C (360°F). Brush a 23-cm (9-in) round springform tin with melted butter. Have the filo sheets ready under a damp-ened clean tea towel (to stop them drying out).

Brush a sheet of filo with melted butter. Drape across the base of prepared tin, letting the edges overhang the sides of the tin. Repeat with another sheet of filo, turning the tin slightly so that this sheet overlaps the first. Repeat with another 4 filo sheets, until tin is evenly lined.

Remove bay leaf from the rice mixture and stir in the slivered almonds. Spoon the rice into the prepared tin.

Cut the remaining filo sheets into 23-cm (9-in) rounds. Brush each round with butter, then layer together three of the rounds and do the same with the remaining three, so you have two separate piles. Place one layered round on top of the rice mixture and brush with butter. Fold in the overhanging pastry to cover, brushing lightly with butter in between each layer. Place the remaining layered filo round on top and brush with butter.

Bake for 30–40 minutes, until pastry is golden. Rest in tin for 10 minutes, then remove springform ring. Cut into wedges to serve.

Pita Bread

Khoubiz

Makes 12

2 teaspoons (7 g/¼ oz) dried
  yeast

pinch of caster sugar

1 cup (250 ml/8½ oz) warm
  water

3 cups (450 g/1 lb) plain flour

½ teaspoon salt

1 tablespoon (20 ml/¾ fl oz)
  olive oil

In a small bowl dissolve the yeast and sugar in half the warm water. Set aside in a warm place for 10 minutes, until the surface becomes frothy.

Meanwhile, sift the flour and salt into the bowl of an electric mixer fitted with the dough hook attachment. Add the yeast mixture, the remaining water and the oil, and knead on the lowest speed for 5 minutes (or by hand for 10 minutes), until smooth and elastic. Place dough in an oiled bowl and turn to coat all over with oil. Cover with cling wrap or a damp tea towel and set aside in a warm place for about 1½ hours or until doubled in size (the first proving).

Preheat the oven to 250°C (480°F). Place two baking trays in oven to heat.

Punch dough down, turn out onto a floured surface and knead for 1 minute. Divide the dough into 12 portions and shape into balls. Roll out each ball into a 15-cm (6-in) round (you may need to lightly flour the work surface and rolling pin to prevent dough sticking). Place rounds 5 cm (2 in) apart on a lightly floured board or upside-down tray, cover with a cloth and leave for 10 minutes to rise.

Dip a thickly folded piece of paper towel in oil and rub the baking trays with oil. Cook the bread in batches: slide the dough rounds onto the hot baking trays and bake in a preheated oven for 6–8 minutes or until bread is puffed up like a balloon. Remove from oven and wrap in a tea towel draped over a wire rack, to keep them warm and soft while you bake the remaining rounds.

&ɔ For wholemeal pita, replace the plain flour with 2 cups wholemeal flour and 1 cup unbleached plain flour.

&ɔ For flatbread with za'atar, brush dough rounds with olive oil and sprinkle with za'atar (page 244) before baking. Bake for 4–5 minutes, until lightly coloured.

Egg & Spinach Nest Bread

Makes 6

2 tablespoons (40 ml/1½ fl oz)
  olive oil

200 g (7 oz) spinach leaves

salt and freshly ground black
  pepper

1 quantity pita bread dough
  (page 92), after first proving

6 eggs

2 tablespoons (40 ml/1½ fl oz)
  paprika oil (page 242)

Preheat the oven to 250°C (480°F). Lightly oil a baking tray.

Heat oil in a large non-stick frying pan over medium heat. Add the spinach
and stir until leaves have wilted and any moisture has evaporated. Season
to taste with salt and pepper.

Punch down the bread dough, turn out onto a floured surface and knead
for 1 minute. Divide dough into six portions and shape into balls. With
lightly floured hands, gently press out each ball into a 10-cm (4-in) round,
and make a depression in the centre to form a nest shape.

Place rounds on prepared baking tray (allow room for spreading), spread
each with spinach and break an egg into the hollow. Bake for 4–5 minutes,
until puffed and golden around the edges. Drizzle paprika oil over the top
and serve hot as a snack, or for breakfast.

Spiced Rusks

Makes 15–18

2 teaspoons (7 g/¼ oz) dried
  yeast

½ teaspoon sugar

about ½ cup (125 ml/4 fl oz)
  luke-warm water

450 g (1 lb) plain flour

1 teaspoon salt

1 teaspoon ground cumin

1 teaspoon ground coriander

2 teaspoons cumin seeds

125 g (4½ oz) unsalted butter,
  melted and allowed to cool

olive oil for brushing

fragrant salt (page 239)

thin slices bastourma, to serve

Dissolve the yeast and sugar in half the water. Leave for 10 minutes in a warm place until bubbles form on the surface.

Sift flour, salt and ground spices into the bowl of an electric mixer fitted with a dough hook, and stir in the cumin seeds. Add the yeast liquid and melted butter. Then, with the mixer on the lowest speed, gradually add just enough of the remaining water to make a stiff dough. Continue kneading on the lowest setting for 10 minutes, until the dough is soft and elastic. Oil a bowl, add dough and turn until coated with oil. Cover the bowl with cling wrap and place in a warm place for 1½–2 hours, until doubled in size.

Preheat the oven to 180°C (360°). Brush two baking trays with oil.

Punch down the dough and knead by hand for 1 minute. Take walnut-sized pieces of dough and roll into snakes about 12 cm (5 in) long. Transfer to baking trays, cover with a damp cloth and leave for 15 minutes.

Brush dough pieces lightly with oil and sprinkle with the fragrant salt. Bake in preheated oven for 20 minutes, then reduce heat to 150°C (300°F) and bake for a further hour until golden. When cool, store rusks in an airtight container for up to a week.

Serve wrapped in thin slices of bastourma.

- Traditionally the dough lengths are coated in sesame seeds (rather than salt) and left in the oven until completely crisp.
- Bastourma is an air-dried beef available from Middle Eastern food stores and some good delicatessens.

Lamb Dumplings
in Yoghurt Sauce

Serves 6–8

olive oil, for brushing

DOUGH

2 cups (300 g/10½ oz) plain flour

½ teaspoon salt

LAMB FILLING

1 tablespoon (20 ml/¾ fl oz) olive oil

½ small onion, finely chopped

225 g (½ lb) lean lamb mince

2 tablespoons pine nuts

¼ teaspoon ground allspice

pinch of ground cinnamon

salt and freshly ground black pepper

YOGHURT SAUCE

1 tablespoon samneh or ghee

2 cloves garlic, crushed with 1 teaspoon sea salt

2 teaspoons dried mint

1 tablespoon (15 g/½ oz) cornflour

1 L (34 fl oz) Greek-style yoghurt

1 egg, lightly beaten

1 cup (250 ml/8½ fl oz) chicken stock

1 teaspoon salt

To make dough, sift flour and salt into a large bowl and make a well in the centre. Pour in ¾ cup (185 ml/6 fl oz) cold water and mix to a soft dough, adding extra flour if necessary. Knead for 3 minutes until smooth. Cover dough with cling wrap and set aside to rest for 30 minutes. >

For the filling, heat the oil in a frying pan over medium heat and cook onion for 5 minutes, until softened. Increase heat to high, add lamb and cook for 5 minutes, breaking up any lumps. Add pine nuts and spices, and season. Cook for a further 2–3 minutes or until all liquid has evaporated. Set aside.

Preheat the oven to 180°C (360°F). Brush two baking trays with oil.

Roll out dough very thinly on a lightly floured surface and cut into 5-cm (2-in) rounds. Place a teaspoon of filling in the centre of each round, fold dough over to form a crescent shape, then press edges together to seal. Transfer to the prepared baking trays, brush with oil and bake for about 12 minutes, until lightly golden but not cooked through.

For the sauce, heat samneh or ghee in a small saucepan over low heat, add garlic and sauté for a minute (don't let it colour). Remove from heat, stir in mint and set aside. Meanwhile, combine cornflour with 2 tablespoons (40 ml/1½ fl oz) water. Put yoghurt in a large saucepan, then whisk in the egg, cornflour mixture and stock. Place over low–medium heat and bring to a gentle simmer, stirring constantly in one direction for 10 minutes until thickened. Add the dumplings and simmer for 5 minutes, to cook through. Stir in the garlic–mint mixture and serve immediately. This ancient dish is traditionally served with rice, but is a hearty meal on its own.

ℰ The dumplings can be made a day ahead (refrigerate covered).

Middle Eastern Grilled Sandwiches

Makes 6

2 tablespoons (40 ml/1½ fl oz) olive oil, plus extra for brushing

1 onion, finely chopped

400 g (14 oz) lamb or beef mince

1 clove garlic, crushed with ½ teaspoon salt

1 fresh red chilli, deseeded and finely diced

1 teaspoon ground cumin

1 teaspoon ground allspice

2 teaspoons sumac

3 tablespoons chopped fresh coriander

3 tablespoons chopped fresh flat-leaf parsley

6 small rounds pita bread

150 g (5 oz) grated haloumi cheese (or use fetta)

Heat oil in a frying pan over medium heat. Add onion and cook for about 5 minutes until softened. Add mince and cook for 5–10 minutes until browned, breaking up any lumps. Add the garlic, chilli, spices and herbs, and stir for 1 minute. Remove from heat and cool for 5–10 minutes.

For each pita round, insert a sharp knife into the edge and cut halfway around, to form a pocket. Divide the meat filling between the pockets, spreading it out evenly, and scatter the filling with some grated haloumi. Close the pita and brush each side with olive oil. Cook on preheated grill (or use a sandwich-maker) until both sides are lightly golden.

Serve hot, cut into wedges. Delicious with tahini dip (page 31).

Lamb & Pine-nut Pastry Rolls

Makes about 30

2 tablespoons (40 ml/1½ fl oz) olive oil

1 onion, finely chopped

400 g (14 oz) lamb mince

2 cloves garlic, crushed with 1 teaspoon salt

1 tablespoon baharat (page 237)

1 teaspoon ground cumin

1 tablespoon sumac

3 tablespoons chopped fresh coriander

1 tablespoon chopped fresh mint

⅓ cup toasted pine nuts

10 sheets filo pastry

⅔ cup (80 ml/3 fl oz) melted unsalted butter

pomegranate molasses, for drizzling

Heat the olive oil in a large frying pan over medium heat. Add the onion and cook for 5 minutes until softened. Increase heat a little, add the lamb and cook for 5–10 minutes until browned, using a wooden spoon to break up any lumps. Add the garlic, spices, coriander, mint and pine nuts, and stir for 1 minute. Remove from heat and allow mixture to cool for 10 minutes.

Preheat oven to 200°C (390°F). Line two baking trays with baking paper.

Cut filo sheets crossways into three equal strips about 12 cm (5 in) wide. (Work with one sheet at a time, covering the remainder with a damp tea towel, to prevent the pastry drying out.) >

Brush pastry strip lightly with melted butter and place a heaped tablespoon of the lamb mixture in a line at one end. Fold pastry edge over filling, fold in sides about 1 cm (⅜ in) and press down to seal, then roll up into a large cigar shape. Keep finished rolls covered with a damp tea towel while you make the rest.

Place rolls on baking trays and brush with melted butter. Bake in preheated oven for 10–15 minutes, until golden-brown. Serve hot, drizzled with a little pomegranate molasses.

Haloumi Bread Rolls

Makes 12

1 quantity sesame bread
 dough (page 110), after first
 proving

180 g (6½ oz) haloumi cheese,
 coarsely grated

1 teaspoon cumin seeds

milk for glazing

Preheat the oven to 200°C (390°F). Brush a baking tray with oil.

Knock down the dough and knead for 1 minute on a lightly floured board. Divide dough into 12 even portions and press each one out to a square shape 5 mm (¼ in) thick. Spread the cheese and cumin seeds over each square and roll up into log shapes. Seal the open ends then tuck ends underneath, forming the dough into an oval shape.

Place dough ovals on baking tray in three rows, join side down, allowing room for spreading. Cut a diagonal slash across the top of each with a sharp knife. Leave in a warm place for 20–30 minutes or until doubled in bulk.

Brush tops lightly with milk and bake for 25–30 minutes or until golden. Transfer to a wire rack to cool slightly, and serve warm.

Lamb, Tomato & Pine-nut Pizza

Makes 6

PIZZA DOUGH

2 teaspoons (7 g/¼ oz) dried yeast

1 cup (250 ml/8½ fl oz) warm water

2 tablespoons (40 ml/1½ fl oz) extra-virgin olive oil

1 teaspoon salt

3 cups (450 g/1 lb) plain flour

LAMB TOPPING

2 tablespoons (40 ml/1½ fl oz) olive oil

1 onion, finely chopped

250 g (9 oz) lean lamb mince (ask butcher to mince leg meat for you)

1 tomato, deseeded and chopped

2 tablespoons tomato paste

¼ cup toasted pine nuts

½ teaspoon ground allspice

¼ teaspoon ground cloves

¼ teaspoon dried chilli flakes (optional)

½ teaspoon salt

¼ teaspoon freshly ground black pepper

2 teaspoons pomegranate molasses

TO SERVE

1 cup fresh flat-leaf parsley leaves

½ cup (125 ml/4 fl oz) Greek-style yoghurt

1 teaspoon sumac

To make the dough, combine yeast and half the water in the bowl of an electric mixer with dough hook fitted, and set aside in a warm place for 10 minutes. >

To the yeast, add the remaining water, the oil, salt and flour, and knead on the lowest speed for 5 minutes (or by hand for 10 minutes), until smooth and elastic. Place dough in an oiled bowl, cover with cling wrap and set aside in a warm place for about 1½ hours, until doubled in bulk.

Meanwhile, prepare the topping. Heat the oil in a non-stick frying pan over medium heat and sauté onion for 10 minutes, until softened and golden. Add the lamb and cook, using a wooden spoon to break up any lumps, until browned. Stir in the remaining topping ingredients, reduce heat to low and cook for 5 minutes. Remove from heat and set aside to cool slightly.

Preheat the oven to 230°C (445°F). Brush three baking trays with oil.

Divide dough into six pieces and roll out on a floured surface to make rounds about 3 mm (⅛ in) thick. Transfer rounds to the baking trays, leaving room for spreading, and set aside to rest for 10 minutes.

Spread some of the lamb topping over each dough round and bake in the preheated oven for 10 minutes, or until edges are golden-brown.

Serve hot, topped with a scattering of parsley, a dollop of yoghurt and a sprinkle of sumac.

Lamb Pies with Herb Labne

Sfiha

Makes 25–30

1 quantity pita bread dough
(page 92), after first proving

1 quantity lamb pizza topping
(page 107)

olive oil, for brushing

about 15 labne balls (see note
page 238)

3 tablespoons finely chopped
fresh mint or flat-leaf parsley

fresh pomegranate seeds, for
garnish (when in season)

Preheat the oven to 200°C (390°F). Lightly oil three baking trays.

Take walnut-sized pieces of dough and roll out on a floured surface to form 8-cm (3-in) rounds. Place a heaped teaspoon of lamb mixture in the centre, brush edges lightly with water, then pinch dough together in four places around the edge, to form a 'basket'. Brush meat and dough edges lightly with oil. Bake pies in preheated oven for 10–12 minutes until golden around the edges.

Meanwhile, drain excess oil from the labne balls and roll each in chopped mint or parsley.

Serve pies hot or warm, topped with half a labne ball. Scatter with fresh pomegranate seeds, if available.

&) In Syria and Lebanon these pies are often made with pastry rather than bread dough.

Sesame Bread Rings

Semit

Makes 15

2 teaspoons (7 g/½ oz) dried yeast

2 teaspoons sugar

¾ cup (180 ml/6 fl oz) warm water

3⅓ cups (500 g/1 lb 2 oz) plain flour

½ cup (125 ml/4 fl oz) milk

1 teaspoon salt

1 tablespoon (20 ml/¾ fl oz) oil

1 egg, lightly beaten with 1 tablespoon water

about 1½ cups sesame seeds

Combine yeast and sugar in ½ cup (125 ml/4 fl oz) of the warm water and stir until dissolved. Stir in enough of the flour to form a paste (about ½ cup), then stir in the milk until you have a thick liquid. Set aside for 10 minutes in a warm place, until the surface becomes frothy.

Sift 2½ cups (375 g/13 oz) of the flour, plus the salt, into the bowl of an electric mixer fitted with a dough hook and make a well in the centre. Pour in the yeast liquid, oil, and remaining water, and knead for 5 minutes on the lowest setting (or 10 minutes by hand), making sure all the flour is incorporated. Add the remaining flour if the dough is sticky and continue kneading until dough is soft, smooth and satiny. Shape the dough into a ball. Oil a large bowl, add dough ball and roll to coat all over in oil. Cover bowl with cling wrap and leave in a warm place for 30–45 minutes, until doubled in bulk (the first proving).

Preheat the oven to 220°C (420°F). Lightly oil two baking trays.

Spread the sesame seeds on a plate. Punch down the dough, turn out onto a lightly floured surface and knead for 1 minute. Divide dough into 15 pieces and roll into snakes 15 cm × 1.5 cm (6 in × ⅝ in). Form each length into a ring, pressing the ends together, brush with the egg wash and then dip the upper surface into sesame seeds. Transfer rings to prepared baking trays, allowing room for spreading, cover loosely with cling wrap and leave to rise in a warm place for 30 minutes, or until doubled in size.

Place a shallow bowl of water in the bottom of the preheated oven. Bake rings for 10 minutes, then reduce temperature to 160°C (320°F) and bake for a further 15–20 minutes or until rings are golden and sound hollow when tapped on the base.

Serve fresh, with goat's cheese or with extra-virgin olive oil and za'atar (page 244).

Vegetables

Vegetables have always had a central place on the Middle Eastern table. Dishes such as ful medames (slow-cooked beans) date back many centuries, as does the fancifully named imam bayaldi (the imam swooned): one of the many explanations for this recipe's title is that an imam's cook prepared stuffed eggplants for his gourmand employer, who was so impressed that he continued eating until he fainted.

Vegetables are enjoyed fried, steamed or in stews, always married with complementing flavours and textures. Often they are stuffed with aromatic rice or other fillings and then baked (as in the stuffed red onions, which have a Persian-influenced stuffing including dried fruit, tamarind, fresh herbs and spices). Many vegetable dishes can be served either hot or cold, usually with a range of yoghurt or nut sauces.

< Artichokes Stewed with Broad Beans & Carrots (page 114)

Artichokes Stewed with Broad Beans & Carrots

Serves 6

1½ cups shelled broad beans, or 1 cup shelled peas

6 prepared globe artichokes (see note opposite), with about 5 cm (2 in) of stalk left intact

12 baby carrots, trimmed but left whole

1 red onion, cut into 6 wedges

juice of 3 lemons

3 cups (750 ml/25 fl oz) water or vegetable stock

2 bay leaves

1 teaspoon coarsely crushed coriander seeds

3 cloves garlic, finely chopped

1½ teaspoons fresh oregano or sweet marjoram leaves

salt and freshly ground black pepper

extra-virgin olive oil, to serve

Blanch the shelled broad beans or peas for 30 seconds in a large saucepan of boiling water, then drain well. Slip off the skins of the broad beans to reveal the bright-green seeds, and set these aside.

Peel the outer skin from the artichoke stalks, then cut each artichoke into quarters lengthways. Place artichokes, carrots, onion, lemon juice, water or stock, bay leaves, coriander seeds, garlic and oregano or marjoram in a large saucepan over high heat. Bring to the boil, then reduce heat and simmer for 15 minutes. Add the broad beans and simmer for 5 minutes.

Season to taste with salt and pepper. Remove from heat and set aside to cool slightly.

Ladle the stew into a serving bowl and drizzle with extra-virgin olive oil. Serve warm or at room temperature.

න To prepare artichokes, tear off the tough outer leaves until only the tender pale-green leaves remain. Using a serrated knife or scissors, slice off the top one-third of the leaves and trim any torn edges. Use a teaspoon to scoop out the hairy 'choke' at the base of the heart, and discard. Place artichokes in a bowl of water with lemon juice added, until needed (this stops them discolouring).

Slow-cooked Brown Beans

Ful medames

Serves 6

1½ cups dried Egyptian brown beans (ful)

¼ cup dried red lentils

2 cloves garlic, crushed with 1 teaspoon salt

freshly ground black pepper

3 tablespoons chopped fresh parsley

ACCOMPANIMENTS

3 tablespoons (60 ml/2 fl oz) olive oil, for drizzling

2 hard-boiled eggs, coarsely chopped (optional)

3 spring onions, thinly sliced (or ½ red onion, thinly sliced)

3 firm ripe tomatoes, diced

2 tablespoons ground cumin

2 lemons, cut into wedges

tahini sauce (see note page 31)

flatbread

Place beans in a large bowl and cover generously with cold water. Leave to soak overnight, then drain.

Place drained beans and the lentils in a large saucepan and add enough cold water to cover them by 2.5 cm (1 in). Place over high heat and bring to the boil, then reduce heat and simmer gently for 1½–2 hours, or until the beans and lentils are tender. (Add more water if needed, to prevent beans from catching on the saucepan base.)

Meanwhile, arrange the accompaniments on a platter or in individual bowls. When beans are cooked, stir in the garlic and season with pepper. Ladle beans into bowls and sprinkle with parsley. Serve with accompaniments in the centre of the table, for diners to help themselves.

❧ This dish is eaten just about anywhere, any time (including breakfast) in Egypt. Egyptian brown beans (ful) are available in Middle Eastern food stores and good delis. You can substitute dried broad (fava) beans.

Eggplant Filled with Lamb

Serves 4

4 long eggplants (each about 250 g/9 oz)

450 g (1 lb) lean lamb mince

1 onion, finely chopped

2 tablespoons finely chopped fresh parsley

½ teaspoon ground allspice or cinnamon

freshly ground black pepper

3 tablespoons tomato paste

2 tablespoons (40 ml/1½ fl oz) olive oil

mixed salad with herbs (page 53) or tomato and cucumber salad with sumac (page 71)

Make a series of deep cuts across each eggplant, at 3-cm (1½-in) intervals along its length. Sprinkle salt into each slit and leave for 30 minutes, then rinse the eggplants and squeeze out excess moisture. Pat dry with paper towels.

Preheat the oven to 180°C (360°F).

To prepare the filling, place lamb, onion, parsley, spices, pepper and 1 teaspoon salt in a bowl and use your hands to mix well. Take some of the mixture and stuff it into the slits in the eggplants, filling generously. Arrange eggplants in a baking dish into which they fit snugly. Mix tomato paste into ⅔ cup (160 ml/5½ fl oz) water and pour over. Drizzle with oil, then bake for 45 minutes, basting occasionally with the juices in the dish.

Serve hot, with your choice of salad.

Stuffed Sweet Chillies

Serves 8

3 tablespoons (60 ml/2 fl oz) olive oil

8 long sweet chillies

1 onion, finely chopped

¾ cup short-grain rice

¼ teaspoon ground allspice

1 × 400-g (14-oz) can chopped tomatoes

½ teaspoon salt

freshly ground black pepper

1 cup chopped fresh flat-leaf parsley

Preheat the oven to 180°C (360°F). Drizzle half the oil over the base of a baking dish large enough to hold all the chillies.

Slice off the stem end of each chilli and scrape out the pith and seeds.

Heat remaining oil in a heavy-based saucepan over medium heat. Add onion and cook 5 minutes until softened. Add rice, stir to coat in the oil and then cook for 2 minutes until translucent. Stir in allspice and half the tomatoes, season with salt and pepper, add ¾ cup (180 ml/6 fl oz) water and bring to the boil. Reduce heat, cover pan and simmer for 10 minutes, or until rice is just cooked. Stir parsley through rice mixture.

Fill each chilli with some of the rice mixture and place on their sides in the baking dish. Combine remaining tomatoes with ¾ cup (180 ml/6 fl oz) water and pour over and around the chillies.

Cover dish with aluminium foil and bake in preheated oven for 30 minutes. Remove foil (add extra water if all liquid has been absorbed) and continue cooking for a further 15 minutes. Serve hot or cold.

∞ You can also use this filling to stuff tomatoes. Slice the tops off 8 large tomatoes, deseed, and hollow out the centres (the flesh can be added to the cooking liquid) and proceed as above.

Stuffed Artichoke Hearts

Serves 8

2 tablespoons (40 ml/1½ fl oz) olive oil

1 onion, finely chopped

2 tablespoons pine nuts

450 g (1 lb) beef mince

½ teaspoon ground cinnamon

2 teaspoons dried mint

½ cup fresh flat-leaf parsley

1 clove garlic, crushed with ½ teaspoon salt

1 egg

2 slices fresh bread, processed to crumbs

freshly ground black pepper

8 globe artichokes, prepared (see note page 115)

3 cups (750 ml/25 fl oz) passata

1 bay leaf

Preheat the oven to 190°C (375°F).

Heat oil in a non-stick frying pan over medium heat. Sauté the onion for 5 minutes or until softened, then add the pine nuts and cook until lightly golden. Remove from heat and set aside to cool slightly.

Place mince, cinnamon, mint, parsley, garlic, egg, breadcrumbs, pepper and onion mixture in a food processor. Pulse until well combined.

Trim bases of prepared artichoke hearts so they will sit flat. Fill the artichoke centres with the meat mixture, forming it into a mound at the top. Arrange artichokes in a baking dish in which they fit snugly. Pour passata over and around the artichokes, add 1 cup (250 ml/8½ fl oz) water and the bay leaf. Cover with a lightly oiled sheet of aluminium foil and seal edges, then bake in preheated oven for 45–60 minutes until artichokes are tender.

&ര When artichokes are not in season, use 4 red capsicums instead.

Green Omelette

Kuku sabsi

Serves 6

⅓ cup (80 ml/3 fl oz) olive oil

1 leek (white part only), finely chopped

120 g (4 oz) spinach leaves, finely shredded

1 cup finely chopped spring onions

½ cup chopped fresh flat-leaf parsley

½ cup chopped fresh coriander

¼ cup chopped fresh dill

1 tablespoon chopped fresh tarragon

2 tablespoons chopped walnuts

8 eggs

salt and freshly ground black pepper

drained yoghurt (see page 9), to serve

Preheat the oven to 170°C (340°F). Use half the oil to generously grease an ovenproof 23-cm (9-in) frying pan or baking dish.

Heat remaining oil in a large heavy-based frying pan over medium heat. Add leek and cook for 5 minutes until softened. Remove from heat and allow to cool.

In a large bowl, toss together the spinach, spring onions, herbs, walnuts and leek until well mixed. In another bowl, whisk eggs until frothy and season with salt and pepper. Pour eggs over the spinach mixture and toss to combine. >

Pour egg mixture into the prepared pan or dish, and spread evenly. Cover with foil and bake for 30 minutes, then remove the foil and continue baking for a further 15 minutes, or until the eggs are set and top is golden. (Alternatively, brown the omelette under a grill for the last few minutes of cooking, but be careful not to overcook or it will dry out.)

Cut into wedges and serve hot or warm, with yoghurt.

ℰ The omelette (kuku) will keep, covered, in the refrigerator for 2 days. It makes ideal picnic or party food.

Lentils & Rice

Serves 4–6

⅓ cup (80 ml/3 fl oz) olive oil

2 onions, finely sliced

1 cup dried brown lentils

1 teaspoon salt

1 cup long-grain rice

Heat the olive oil in a medium-sized saucepan over low–medium heat. Add onion and cook for 10–15 minutes or until a dark golden-brown. Remove a third of the onion and set aside in a small bowl.

Add the lentils, salt and 1 litre (34 fl oz) water to the remaining onions in the saucepan and increase heat to medium–high. Bring to the boil and cook for 15 minutes, then stir in the rice and reduce heat to low. Continue cooking for another 15 minutes or until all the water is absorbed and the lentils are mushy.

Serve hot or at room temperature, topped with reserved onions. This dish is good on its own with yoghurt, or as an accompaniment for grilled meats or fish.

The Imam Swooned

Imam bayildi

Serves 6

6 slender (Japanese) eggplants

3 tablespoons salt

½ cup (125 ml/4 fl oz) olive oil

3 onions, cut in half and thinly sliced

4 cloves garlic, finely chopped

3 tomatoes, peeled and diced

½ teaspoon dried oregano

3 tablespoons chopped fresh flat-leaf parsley, plus extra for garnish

¼ teaspoon ground allspice

¼ teaspoon ground cinnamon

2 tablespoons (40 ml/1½ fl oz) freshly squeezed lemon juice

1 teaspoon soft brown sugar

salt and freshly ground black pepper

Cut a deep slit along the length of each eggplant, three-quarters of the way through the flesh (leaving the base and stem end intact). Dissolve the salt in 1.5 L (3 pt 3 fl oz) cold water in a large bowl. Add eggplants and leave to soak for 30 minutes. Drain, rinse and gently squeeze out any excess moisture, then pat dry with paper towels.

Heat about 2 tablespoons of the oil in a large frying pan over low–medium heat. Sauté the onions for 15 minutes, until softened and lightly golden. Stir in the garlic and cook for 1 minute, then add the tomatoes and oregano, and simmer for 5 minutes. Stir in the parsley and spices, remove pan from heat and set aside.

Preheat the oven to 180°C (360°F).

Heat about 3 tablespoons oil in another large frying pan over medium-high heat. Add the eggplants and sauté for about 5–8 minutes, turning occasionally until cooked through and the cut edges are golden. Remove from heat and use a teaspoon to gently scoop out flesh from each slit. Chop the flesh and add to the onion–tomato mixture.

Place eggplants, slit side up, in a baking dish just large enough to fit them snugly. Spoon as much filling as possible into the slits, scattering any remainder over the top. Combine ⅓ cup (80 ml/3 fl oz) water with the remaining oil, the lemon juice and the sugar, then drizzle mixture over the eggplants. Cover dish and bake in preheated oven for 20 minutes until tender, adding more water if necessary. Leave to cool to room temperature.

Serve drizzled with the pan juices and garnished with chopped parsley.

ℜ This dish can be made a day ahead: store (covered) in the refrigerator and bring to room temperature to serve.

Okra with Tomatoes & Onions

Serves 4

100 ml (3½ fl oz) olive oil

1 onion, sliced

500 g (1 lb 2 oz) young okra, stems trimmed

2 cloves garlic, finely chopped

1 × 400-g (14-oz) can chopped tomatoes

salt and freshly ground black pepper

juice of 1 lemon

2 tablespoons chopped fresh coriander

Heat the oil in a non-stick frying pan over medium heat. Add the onion and cook for 5 minutes, until softened. Add the okra and garlic, and sauté for 5 minutes. Pour in the can of tomatoes and enough water to just cover all the vegetables. Bring to a simmer and cook for 15–20 minutes until the okra are very tender, then add the lemon juice and cook for another 5 minutes. Stir in the coriander leaves and serve hot or at room temperature.

Often served cold as a meze, this dish is also delicious served hot with a meat or rice dish.

ဆ Okra is available fresh in the warmer months. Choose young specimens no more than 12 cm (5 in) long.

Leek & Pumpkin Patties

Makes 16–18

2 tablespoons (40 ml/1½ fl oz) olive oil, plus extra for brushing

1 leek (white part only), very finely chopped

600 g (1 lb 5 oz) peeled pumpkin, cut into 5-cm (2-in) pieces

1 cup (175 g/6½ oz) fine burghul (cracked wheat)

½ cup finely chopped fresh coriander

¼ cup finely chopped fresh flat-leaf parsley

½ cup (75 g/2½ oz) chickpea flour (besan), plus extra if needed

½ teaspoon ground allspice

½ teaspoon ground cumin

½ teaspoon ground coriander

¼ teaspoon ground ginger (optional)

½ teaspoon salt

freshly ground black pepper

yoghurt or spiced fetta and yoghurt (page 30), to serve

Heat oil in a non-stick frying pan over medium heat. Add leek and cook for 5 minutes until softened. Set aside.

Cook the pumpkin in a large saucepan of boiling salted water for about 10 minutes, until tender. Drain well and leave to cool.

Place burghul in a bowl and cover with cold water. Leave to soak for 5 minutes, then drain well. Tip into a clean tea towel and squeeze out as much water as possible, then transfer to a large bowl. >

Add cooked pumpkin to the burghul, mash roughly together, then stir in the leek, coriander and parsley. Sift the flour, spices, salt and pepper over the vegetable mixture and mix well to combine. (Depending on the moisture content of the pumpkin, you may need to add more flour.) Refrigerate until well chilled.

Preheat the oven to 190°C (375°F). Line two baking trays with baking paper.

With wet hands, take small handfuls of the pumpkin mixture and mould into round patties. Place on baking trays, brush tops with olive oil and bake for 30 minutes or until golden-brown. Serve with yoghurt, or spiced fetta and yoghurt.

⨏ You can prepare the patties (up to baking stage) a day ahead and store, covered, in the fridge.

Fried Eggplant

Serves 4–6

2 medium-sized eggplants

salt

vegetable oil or light olive oil
for shallow-frying

1 cup flat-leaf parsley leaves

1 lemon, cut into wedges

tahini sauce (see note page 31)
or nut sauce (page 243),
to serve

Cut eggplants lengthways into thin (5-mm/¼-in) slices, or into long wedges 1 cm (⅜ in) wide. Spread on a wire rack, sprinkle both sides with salt and leave for 30 minutes. Squeeze each slice to get rid of the bitter juices, rinse under running water and then pat dry with paper towels.

Heat the oil to a depth of 1 cm (⅜ in) in a deep-sided frying pan over high heat. If using a deep-fryer, heat oil to 180°C (360°F). Fry a few eggplant slices at a time, for 3–4 minutes or until golden-brown on both sides. Drain on paper towels.

Deep-fry the parsley leaves for 30 seconds or until crisp, then drain on paper towels.

Serve eggplant garnished with the parsley, with lemon wedges on the side for squeezing, and with one of the suggested sauces alongside.

∽ You can use zucchini instead of the eggplants (no need to salt them).

Silverbeet Rolls

Serves 4

24 large silverbeet leaves

3 tablespoons (60 ml/2 fl oz) olive oil

juice of 1 lemon

FILLING

1 cup long-grain rice

⅓ cup (80 ml/3 fl oz) olive oil

1 onion, finely chopped

1 × 400-g (14-oz) can chickpeas, drained

1 cup chopped fresh flat-leaf parsley

1 cup chopped tomatoes

1 teaspoon salt

freshly ground black pepper

½ teaspoon ground allspice

1 teaspoon dried mint (or 1 tablespoon chopped fresh mint)

3 tablespoons (60 ml/2 fl oz) freshly squeezed lemon juice

For the filling, first rinse the rice until the water runs clear, then drain well and set aside. Heat oil in a frying pan over medium heat. Add the onion and cook for 5 minutes until softened. Transfer onion and oil to a large bowl, add the rice and all the remaining filling ingredients, and mix well.

Cut silverbeet leaves in half lengthways and remove stalks. Line the base of a large saucepan with the stalks. Cut leaves into 10-cm (4-in) squares, dip into hot water to soften, then drain. Place a silverbeet square, shiny side down, on a clean surface, place a tablespoon of filling in the centre, and wrap up into a neat roll. Repeat with remaining leaves and filling.

Place the rolls, seam side down, in layers in the saucepan you have lined with the stems. Drizzle rolls with olive oil and lemon juice, and put a plate on top to keep them in place. Add ½ litre (500 ml/17 fl oz) water, put lid on pan and bring to the boil over medium heat. Reduce heat and simmer gently for 30–45 minutes, until rice is tender. Remove from heat and set aside for 15 minutes before serving warm.

&) You can use vine leaves or cabbage leaves instead of the silverbeet. Prepare vine leaves as for the recipe on page 15. If using cabbage leaves, blanch for 2 minutes in boiling salted water, drain, and remove the tough centre rib.

Deep-fried Cauliflower

Serves 4–6

1 medium-sized cauliflower,
  separated into florets

vegetable oil or light olive oil
  for deep-frying

½ cup plain flour, for coating

2 eggs, lightly beaten

1½ cups fresh breadcrumbs

tahini sauce (see note page 31)
  or yoghurt and garlic sauce
  (see note page 246), to serve

Cook cauliflower in a large saucepan of salted water for 3 minutes. Drain well, then pat dry with paper towels.

Heat the oil to a depth of 5 cm (2 in) in a deep-sided frying pan over high heat. If using a deep-fryer, heat oil to 180°C (360°F).

Place flour, eggs and breadcrumbs on three separate plates. Turn the cauliflower florets in the flour to coat, shaking off any excess. Dip them in the beaten eggs and then into the breadcrumbs, coating well. Deep-fry, in batches, for 4–5 minutes or until golden-brown. Drain on paper towels.

Serve hot with your choice of sauce.

Stuffed Red Onions

Serves 6

walnut-sized piece of tamarind
  pulp

1 cup (250ml/8½ fl oz) boiling
  water

6 medium-sized red onions,
  peeled

200 g (7 oz) lamb or beef
  mince

⅓ cup long-grain rice, washed
  (see page 13)

1½ teaspoons baharat (page
  237)

¼ teaspoon ground turmeric

½ teaspoon salt

freshly ground black pepper

¼ cup sultanas

1 ripe tomato, deseeded and
  chopped

1 tablespoon tomato paste

2 tablespoons chopped fresh
  flat-leaf parsley

2 tablespoons chopped fresh
  mint

2 tablespoons (40 ml/1½ fl oz)
  olive oil

Soak the tamarind pulp in boiling water for 30 minutes. Preheat the oven
to 180°C (360°F).

Bring a large saucepan of salted water to the boil and boil the red onions for
10–12 minutes until just softened. Drain and set aside until cool enough to
handle, then trim just enough off the bases so the onions will sit flat. Take a
1-cm (⅜-in) slice from the top of each onion and carefully remove the centre
layers, leaving a rim of about 1 cm (⅜ in). Reserve the centre and tops. >

Chop the inner onion layers and onion tops finely. Place the chopped onion, meat, rice and remaining ingredients (except tamarind) in a large bowl and use your hands to mix thoroughly. Three-quarters fill each onion with some of the meat mixture.

Transfer onions to a baking dish just large enough to fit them snugly side by side. Pour the tamarind liquid through a sieve to remove any seeds, pressing with the back of a spoon to extract all the pulp, then pour the resulting liquid over the onions. Cover the baking dish with aluminium foil and bake in preheated oven for 50–60 minutes or until onions are very tender and the filling is cooked. (Check occasionally and add extra water if liquid has been absorbed.)

Serve hot, with salads and warmed flatbread.

Green Beans in Olive Oil

Loubia bi zeit

Serves 4

3 tablespoons (60 ml/2 fl oz) olive oil, plus extra to serve

1 onion, finely diced

2 cloves garlic, finely chopped

350 g (12 oz) green beans, topped and tailed

3 firm ripe tomatoes, diced

½ teaspoon salt

freshly ground black pepper

Heat oil in a non-stick frying pan over low–medium heat and cook onion and garlic for 10 minutes, until softened and lightly golden. Add the beans and stir for 1 minute, then add the tomatoes, salt and just enough water to cover the beans. Bring to a simmer and cook for 20–30 minutes until the beans are tender and the sauce has reduced.

Season with pepper to taste and serve hot or at room temperature, drizzled with extra-virgin olive oil.

ဢ This classic Lebanese dish is often served as a meze.

Seafood

Fresh fish is a favoured meal in the coastal regions of the Middle East and around fresh inland waters. In the past, fish was salted and dried to preserve it for long periods, and dried fish is still popular today. Over time local recipes were influenced by those of neighbouring countries who share the waters of the Mediterranean and Gulf seas.

Fried or grilled small fish, particularly sardines, red mullet (in Lebanon known as Sultan Ibrahim, after a famous Muslim ruler) and whitebait, are very popular. Whole larger fish are typically served with sauces made with tahini, or herbs and nuts. The fish curry here is from the gulf states, and, like many recipes from that area, reflects Indian influences (it includes lots of onions, and the dried lime known as loomi).

< Baked Fish with Herb & Walnut Sauce (page 146)

Baked Fish with Herb & Walnut Sauce

Serves 4

1 × 1.2 kg (2 lb 7 oz) whole
snapper, or 4 × baby
snappers, cleaned

salt and freshly ground black
pepper

olive oil for brushing

1 tablespoon pomegranate
seeds (when in season)

HERB & WALNUT SAUCE

½ cup (125 ml/4 fl oz) extra-
virgin olive oil

1 cup walnuts, toasted

2 spring onions (white part
only), chopped

1 cup chopped fresh coriander

2 tablespoons chopped fresh
parsley

2 cloves garlic, chopped

½ teaspoon ground cinnamon

juice of 1 lemon

pinch of ground cayenne
pepper (optional)

Preheat the oven to 180°C (360°F) if using one large fish; if using small fish, preheat to 200°C (390°F). Brush a large baking tray generously with oil.

Pat fish dry with paper towels and use a sharp knife to make three shallow slashes across the body on each side. Season the cuts and body cavity with salt and pepper. Brush fish with olive oil and transfer to the baking tray.

Bake in preheated oven for 30–40 minutes (large fish) or 15 minutes (small fish). When flesh behind the gills pulls easily away, the fish is cooked.

While fish is cooking, make the sauce. Place all the ingredients in a food processor and pulse until well mixed and the walnuts are coarsely chopped. Taste, and add extra lemon juice, salt or pepper if required.

Carefully transfer cooked fish to a platter and spoon sauce over. Garnish with pomegranate seeds, if available. Serve with a refreshing salad such as the citrus and watercress salad (page 54).

Fish Cakes

Serves 4

1½ cups fine burghul (cracked wheat)

1 small onion, chopped

1 cup finely chopped fresh coriander

2 tablespoons finely chopped fresh mint

1 teaspoon ground allspice

finely grated zest of 1 lemon

600 g (1 lb 5 oz) white fish fillets (e.g. snapper, blue eye), cut into pieces

salt and freshly ground black pepper

olive oil for frying

PINE NUT FILLING

3 tablespoons (60 ml/2 fl oz) olive oil

¼ cup pine nuts

2 onions, halved and finely sliced

Place burghul in a sieve and rinse under running water until water runs clear. Place in a bowl and cover with water. Leave to soak for 10 minutes, until grains have swelled. Drain in a sieve and press with the back of a spoon to remove excess moisture.

Place burghul, onion, coriander and mint in a food processor and blend until finely chopped. Add the allspice, lemon zest and fish, then blend until mixture is well combined and paste-like. Season with salt and pepper, and set aside.

For the nut filling, heat the oil in a frying pan over a medium heat. Add the pine nuts and cook for a minute or until golden-brown. Remove with a slotted spoon and drain on paper towels.

Reduce heat, add onions to the pan and cook for 5 minutes or until transparent. Drain on paper towels and mix with the pine nuts.

With wet hands, take a walnut-sized piece of the fish mixture and shape into a ball. Press your thumb into the centre to make a hollow, fill with a little of the nut mixture, then seal and mould back into a ball shape. Press gently to form a flat patty.

Heat 2 cm (¾ in) oil in a deep frying pan over a high heat. Fry the fish cakes for 2 minutes on each side until golden-brown. Drain on paper towels and serve hot with tahini sauce (see note page 31).

§ To save time, you could make the fish cakes without the filling.

Fried Little Fish in Spiced Flour

Samak maqli

Serves 4

oil for deep-frying

2 teaspoons sea salt

500 g (1 lb 2 oz) fresh
whitebait

1 cup (150 g/10½ oz) plain
flour

1 tablespoon (15 g/½ oz)
cornflour

1 teaspoon freshly ground
black pepper

2 teaspoons ground paprika

2 tablespoons finely chopped
fresh flat-leaf parsley

3 lemons, cut into wedges

Pour 5 cm (2 in) oil into a deep-fryer or wok and heat to 190°C (375°F).

Sprinkle salt over fish and toss to season all over. Sift flours, pepper and paprika into a large bowl. Toss fish in the spiced flour (use your hands for this) to coat well, then shake off any excess.

Carefully slide a handful of whitebait into the hot oil. Fry for about 2 minutes until light-golden and crisp, then remove and drain on paper towels. Repeat with remaining fish, working in small batches.

Pile cooked whitebait on a platter, sprinkle with parsley and serve with lemon wedges.

ॐ Small red mullet and sardines can also be cooked this way. Or for a change use green (uncooked) shelled prawns.

Spiced Prawns with Rice

Machbous rubyan

Serves 6

⅓ cup (80 ml/3 fl oz) olive oil

24 large green (raw) prawns, shelled and deveined but tails left intact

1 onion, finely chopped

2 cloves garlic, crushed with 1 teaspoon salt

2 teaspoons baharat (page 237)

½ teaspoon ground turmeric

4 ripe tomatoes, peeled and chopped

2 cups long-grain rice, washed (see page 13)

freshly ground black pepper

¼ cup fresh flat-leaf parsley leaves, for garnish

¼ cup fresh coriander leaves, for garnish

tomato and cucumber salad with sumac (page 71), to serve

Heat half the oil in a large heavy-based saucepan over medium–high heat. Fry prawns, in two batches, for 2 minutes, tossing occasionally until flesh is opaque. Remove and set aside.

Add remaining oil to the saucepan over medium heat. Add onion and cook for 10 minutes, until lightly golden, then add the garlic, baharat and turmeric, stirring for 1 minute. Add the tomatoes, rice, 2½ cups (625 ml/21 fl oz) water and a generous grinding of pepper, cover pan tightly and bring to boil, then reduce heat and simmer for 15 minutes.

Stir the rice mixture and place the prawns on top. Cover pan again and cook for a further 5 minutes or until rice is cooked. Remove from heat, gently stir the prawns into the rice, replace lid and leave for 5 minutes before serving.

Serve scattered with the parsley and coriander leaves, and accompanied with the tomato and cucumber salad with sumac.

Grilled Red Mullet in Vine Leaves

Serves 4

12 large vine leaves, fresh or brined

2 cloves garlic, finely chopped

1 cup finely chopped fresh parsley

sea salt and black pepper

12 small red mullet (or use sardines), cleaned

olive oil for frying

1 lemon, cut into wedges

If using vine leaves preserved in brine, rinse and then soak them in fresh water for 20 minutes. Rinse, soak again in fresh water for 15 minutes, then rinse and pat dry with paper towels. If using fresh vine leaves, plunge into boiling water for 20 seconds, remove, refresh in cold water and pat dry.

Preheat oven grill or barbecue to high. Combine garlic and parsley, and season with salt and pepper. Stuff each fish with some garlic–parsley mixture.

Lay vine leaves flat on a work surface, with vein side facing up. Place one fish in the middle of each leaf and roll up to enclose. Brush parcels with oil and grill or barbecue for 3 minutes on each side until fish flesh is white and leaves are blackened slightly.

Serve immediately, with lemon wedges for squeezing.

℘ If the vine leaves are small, use two (overlapped) leaves per fish.

Squid Stuffed with Rice

Serves 6

12 small squid, cleaned, with tentacles separated and chopped

½ cup fresh flat-leaf parsley leaves, for garnish

2 lemons, cut into wedges

RICE FILLING

2 tablespoons (40 ml/1½ fl oz) olive oil

1 onion, chopped

½ cup short-grain rice

1 clove garlic, crushed with 1 teaspoon salt

¼ cup toasted pine nuts

3 tablespoons chopped fresh flat-leaf parsley

freshly ground black pepper

5 saffron threads, soaked in 1 tablespoon (20 ml/¾ fl oz) warm water

ONION SAUCE

3 tablespoons (60 ml/2 fl oz) olive oil

2 large onions, thinly sliced

2 tablespoons tomato paste

½ teaspoon ground sweet paprika

1 cup (250 ml/8½ fl oz) fish stock or water

3 tablespoons (60 ml/2 fl oz) freshly squeezed lemon juice

For the filling, heat the oil in a heavy-based frying pan over medium heat. Add the onion and sauté for 10 minutes, until soft and lightly golden. Stir in the chopped squid tentacles, rice, garlic, pine nuts, parsley, pepper and saffron (with soaking water), mixing well. Two-thirds fill each squid tube with rice mixture and close the opening with toothpicks or small metal skewers.

To make the sauce, heat oil in a large frying pan over medium heat. Add the sliced onions and cook for 5 minutes until softened. Reduce heat to low, cover onions with a piece of baking paper and continue cooking for 10–15 minutes until soft and a deep-golden colour. Stir in tomato paste and paprika.

Arrange stuffed squid over the onions and pour in the stock or water. Bring to the boil, cover, then reduce heat and simmer gently for 20 minutes. Stir in lemon juice and continue to simmer, uncovered, for 2 minutes until sauce is reduced and squid is tender.

Serve hot, garnished with the parsley and lemon wedges.

ℵ Choose squid with tubes about 12 cm (5 in) long.

Prawns Grilled with Thyme & Spices

Serves 4

12 green (raw) king prawns, butterflied

1 teaspoon coriander seeds

3 tablespoons (60 ml/2 fl oz) olive oil

finely grated zest of ½ lemon

1 tablespoon chopped fresh thyme

1 teaspoon sumac

1 tablespoon za'atar (page 244)

Lay the prawns, shell side down, on a baking tray.

Preheat barbecue grill or grill pan to high.

Crush coriander seeds coarsely in a mortar. Combine in a small bowl with the oil, lemon zest, thyme, sumac and za'atar. Spread this mixture over the prawns, then slide onto the hot grill, shell side down, and cook for about 6 minutes, until the flesh is opaque. Serve immediately.

Fish Curry

Serves 6

⅓ cup (80 ml/3 fl oz) olive oil

2 onions, thinly sliced

1 teaspoon grated fresh ginger

2 cloves garlic, crushed with
1 teaspoon salt

½ teaspoon dried chilli flakes

1 teaspoon baharat (page 237)

½ teaspoon ground turmeric

3 tomatoes, peeled and
chopped

1 tablespoon tomato paste

1 cinnamon stick

2 loomi (dried limes), pierced
with a skewer in several
places

6 × 180-g (6½-oz) firm white
fish cutlets (e.g. snapper,
barramundi)

about ½ cup fresh coriander
leaves, for garnish

Heat half the oil in a deep frying pan over medium heat. Add the onion and sauté for 5 minutes. Stir in ginger, garlic, chilli and ground spices, and cook for 1 minute. Add tomatoes, tomato paste, cinnamon stick, loomi and 1 cup (250 ml/8½ fl oz) water, cover and simmer 15 minutes.

Meanwhile, heat the remaining oil in a frying pan over high heat. Add the fish cutlets and cook for 1 minute on each side to seal and brown a little. Carefully transfer fish to the sauce, in a single layer, replace lid and simmer gently for about 10 minutes until fish is cooked through.

Garnish with coriander leaves and serve with rice.

Fish Kebabs

Makes 8

⅓ cup (80 ml/3 fl oz) olive oil

½ teaspoon freshly ground black pepper

2 tablespoons (40 ml/1½ fl oz) freshly squeezed lemon juice

½ teaspoon ground allspice

2 bay leaves, broken into pieces

800 g (1 lb 12oz) blue eye, ocean trout or other firm-fleshed fish, cut into 3-cm (1¼-in) cubes

sea salt

You will need eight 20-cm (8-in) skewers: if using bamboo skewers, soak in lemon juice or water for 20 minutes before threading.

Combine the oil, pepper, lemon juice, allspice and bay leaves in a large bowl. Add the cubed fish and toss to coat well in the marinade. Cover, and refrigerate for 2–3 hours, stirring occasionally.

Preheat barbecue or grill to high.

Thread fish onto skewers, reserving marinade. Grill for 8–10 minutes, turning and basting with marinade occasionally (when cooked, the flesh will flake easily). Serve kebabs immediately, sprinkled with sea salt and accompanied with babaganouj (page 18) or yoghurt, lemon and mint sauce (page 246).

ঙ A lemony salad such as tabbouleh (page 70) goes well with these kebabs.

Poultry

In the Middle East in past times, chickens were kept chiefly for producing eggs and were only eaten on special occasions. Duck was another festive dish; in Egypt, goose was the specialty.

Today chicken, duck and pigeon are still popular for celebrations, whether roasted with a spicy stuffing or made into an elaborate soup. A stuffed chicken will generally feature on the table at a feast: in Iraq the filling is likely to include burghul and vegetables, or lamb and nuts; in Iran, a combination of dried fruits and spices; in the gulf states, rice and pine nuts are popular. Cold dishes such as Circassian chicken are also ideal to serve as part of a buffet. In the everyday kitchen, chicken is often found marinating in herbs, spices and lemon juice in readiness for grilling. Quail also marries well with Middle Eastern spices.

< Grilled Quail with Tomato & Saffron (page 164)

Grilled Quail with Tomato & Saffron

Serves 6

6 large quail, butterflied

⅓ cup (80 ml/3 fl oz) olive oil

1 onion, roughly chopped

2 tomatoes, chopped

2 tablespoons (40 ml/1½ fl oz) freshly squeezed lime juice

freshly ground black pepper

½ teaspoon baharat (page 237)

pinch of saffron threads

yoghurt, to serve

Place quail in a large ceramic dish.

Place all the remaining ingredients (except yoghurt) in the bowl of a food processor and blend until well combined. Pour this marinade over the quail, turning to coat both sides well. Cover and refrigerate for at least 2 hours, or overnight, turning occasionally.

Heat a barbecue or grill to medium–high.

Thread two skewers through each quail, crossways from one side to the other, to help keep them flat during cooking. Grill quail for 3–5 minutes on each side until golden-brown and cooked through, basting occasionally with any remaining marinade.

Serve hot, with yoghurt and a salad. Sweet and sour eggplant salad (page 65) goes well with this dish.

Duck Fillet in Walnut & Pomegranate Sauce

Serves 4

2 teaspoons fragrant salt (page 239)

pinch of ground cinnamon

1 tablespoon (20 ml/¾ fl oz) olive oil

4 duck breast fillets (skin on), excess fat removed

WALNUT & POMEGRANATE SAUCE

2 tablespoons samneh

2 shallots, finely chopped

¾ cup ground walnuts

1 tablespoon (20 ml/¾ fl oz) pomegranate molasses

1½ cups (375 ml/12 fl oz) chicken stock

1 tablespoon honey, or to taste

3 cardamom pods, cracked

1 cinnamon stick

freshly squeezed lemon juice (optional)

¼ cup walnut halves, roasted and roughly chopped

fresh pomegranate seeds (when in season), for garnish

Preheat the oven to 190°C (375°F). Line a baking tray with baking paper. Combine the fragrant salt with the ground cinnamon and set aside.

Heat the oil in a heavy-based frying pan over high heat. Put in the duck breasts skin side down and cook for 2 minutes. Turn, and cook for another minute. Remove duck breasts from the pan and rub the fragrant salt mix over the skin. >

Place duck breasts, skin side down, on the baking tray and bake in the preheated oven for 5 minutes. Remove from oven and set aside to rest for 10 minutes.

To make the sauce, melt samneh in a heavy-based frying pan over medium heat. Sauté shallots for 3–5 minutes, until softened and translucent. Stir in the walnuts and cook for a minute, then add the pomegranate molasses, stock, honey, cardamom and cinnamon, and bring to the boil. Simmer for 5 minutes, until it forms a sauce consistency. Adjust seasoning, adding lemon juice or more honey to achieve a sweet–sour balance.

Serve duck with the sauce spooned over and garnished with chopped walnuts and pomegranate seeds (when available). Chelou (page 75) or burghul pilaf (page 81) are good accompaniments.

☙ If pomegranates are not in season, you can substitute dried cranberries.

Chicken Eggah

⅓ cup (80 ml/3 fl oz) olive oil

1 leek (white part only), finely chopped

450 g (1 lb) chicken mince

salt and freshly ground black pepper

½ teaspoon ground allspice

½ teaspoon ground cardamom

3 tablespoons chopped fresh coriander or flat-leaf parsley

6 eggs, beaten

Heat half the oil in a non-stick frying pan over low–medium heat. Add leek and sauté for 10 minutes until lightly golden. Stir in the chicken and sauté until turning white, using a wooden spoon to break up any lumps. Stir in the salt, pepper, spices and chopped herbs. Add chicken mixture to the eggs and stir to combine well.

Heat remaining oil in a clean frying pan over medium heat. Pour in the egg and chicken mixture, spreading it evenly over the base of the pan. Reduce the heat to low, cover pan and cook for 15 minutes, or until the eggs have set and the top is still a little runny. Place pan under a hot grill for 2–3 minutes until the top is set and golden. Gently shake pan to loosen eggah, then slide it onto a plate. Serve hot or cold, cut into wedges.

ℬ There are infinite versions of this cake-like omelette (also called a kuku – see recipe page 125), but all are bursting with flavour.

Circassian Chicken

Serves 4

1 × 1.3-kg (2 lb 14-oz) chicken

1 onion, quartered

2 sticks celery, roughly
chopped

1 carrot, roughly chopped

2 bay leaves

4 parsley stalks

6 black peppercorns

2 teaspoons ground paprika

about 2 tablespoons (40 ml/
1½ fl oz) walnut oil

250 g (9 oz) walnuts, plus
extra for garnish

2 slices stale white bread

2 cloves garlic, chopped

salt and ground white pepper

Place chicken, onion, celery, carrot, bay leaves, parsley and peppercorns in a large saucepan and cover generously with water. Bring to the boil, then reduce heat and simmer (uncovered) for 1 hour, removing any scum that rises to the surface.

Remove pan from the heat and set aside until chicken is cool enough to handle. Separate the meat from the bones, returning the bones to the saucepan, discarding the skin and reserving the meat. Return pan to heat, bring the stock back to the boil and cook until it has reduced by half. Strain and reserve the stock, discarding the bones.

Meanwhile, shred the meat. In a bowl, toss the meat with about 3 table-spoons of the stock, to keep it moist. Mix half the paprika with the walnut oil and set aside for 10 minutes.

Blend the walnuts in a food processor until coarsely ground. Soak the bread in ½ cup (125 ml/4 fl oz) stock, add to the processor bowl and process to a paste. Add remaining paprika, the garlic, salt and pepper, and continue to process while gradually adding 1 cup (250 ml/8½ fl oz) stock to make a smooth sauce of pouring consistency. Season to taste.

Toss the chicken with half the walnut sauce. Spoon onto a serving platter and drizzle the remaining sauce over. Serve cold, drizzled with paprika oil and garnished with extra walnuts.

🔊 Walnut oil is available from health-food stores, delis and some supermarkets.

Grilled Lemony Chicken

1 onion

⅓ cup (80 ml/2¾ fl oz) freshly squeezed lemon juice

1 clove garlic, crushed with 1 teaspoon salt

freshly ground black pepper

2 teaspoons dried mint or oregano

12 chicken thighs on the bone

3 tablespoons (60 ml/2 fl oz) melted unsalted butter or samneh

1 teaspoon ground sweet paprika

Grate the onion over a bowl to capture all the juices and flesh. Add the lemon juice, garlic, pepper and mint or oregano, and stir to combine. Add chicken and toss to coat. Cover and refrigerate for 2–6 hours (overnight is even better).

Preheat a barbecue or grill to medium–high.

Combine the melted butter or samneh with the paprika. Remove chicken from marinade, draining off any excess, and brush all over with the flavoured butter. Cook on preheated grill for 6–8 minutes on each side, until golden-brown and cooked through, basting frequently with the butter.

Serve with plain rice and a fresh salad such as the mixed salad with herbs (page 53).

Iraqi Roast Stuffed Chicken

Dajaj al timman

Serves 6

½ cup long-grain rice

2 tablespoons samneh, plus extra for brushing

1 onion, finely chopped

50 g (1¾ oz) chicken livers, cleaned (optional)

¼ cup pine nuts

¼ cup chopped walnuts

2 tablespoons sultanas

½ teaspoon baharat (page 237)

½ teaspoon salt

freshly ground black pepper

1 × 1.8-kg (4-lb) chicken

½ cup (125 ml/4 fl oz) chicken stock

Preheat the oven to 180°C (360°F). Place rice in a sieve and rinse until the water runs clear. Drain well.

Heat samneh in a heavy-based saucepan over a medium heat. Add onion and sauté for 5–8 minutes, until lightly golden. Add the chicken livers (if using), pine nuts and walnuts, and cook for 2 minutes. Stir in the rice and cook for a further 3 minutes.

Stir in the sultanas, baharat, 1 cup (250 ml/8½ fl oz) water, and salt and pepper. Increase heat to high, cover pan, bring to the boil, then reduce heat and simmer for 10 minutes or until the water has been absorbed. Remove from the heat and set aside, still covered. >

Rinse the chicken and pat dry with paper towels. Spoon the rice mixture into the cavity and secure with a skewer (or truss the chicken with string). Place on a rack in a roasting dish, brush with some melted samneh and season with salt and pepper. Pour the stock into the dish and bake in pre-heated oven for 1½ hours, basting occasionally. The chicken is cooked if juices run clear when pierced with a skewer between the leg and body.

Cut chicken into portions, and serve with the rice filling alongside and a crisp salad.

Chicken-liver Kebabs

Makes about 12

800 g (1 lb 12 oz) chicken livers, any sinews removed

100 ml (3½ fl oz) olive oil

1 tablespoon (20 ml/¾ fl oz) pomegranate molasses

1 clove garlic, crushed with ½ teaspoon salt

finely grated zest of 1 lemon

1 teaspoon fresh thyme leaves

olive oil for frying

fragrant salt (page 239), for garnish

yoghurt, lemon and mint sauce (page 246), to serve

If using bamboo skewers, soak in water for at least 20 minutes before use, to prevent them burning. Meanwhile, place livers in a colander and rinse under cold water. Drain, then pat dry with paper towels.

Combine 3 tablespoons (60 ml/2 fl oz) oil, the pomegranate molasses, garlic, lemon zest and thyme in a glass or ceramic bowl. Add livers and turn to coat thoroughly. Leave to marinate for 1–2 hours in the refrigerator.

Thread livers onto skewers. Heat remaining oil in a large frying pan over medium–high heat and fry the kebabs for 4–5 minutes, turning once, until just firm (the liver should still be pink in the centre).

Serve hot, sprinkled with fragrant salt and with a bowl of yoghurt, lemon and mint sauce alongside.

Skewered Chicken Pieces

Makes 12

4 lemons

3 tablespoons (60 ml/2 fl oz) extra-virgin olive oil

1 red onion, cut into 6 wedges and layers separated

12 fresh bay leaves

2 teaspoons dried oregano

salt and freshly ground black pepper, to taste

4 skinless chicken breast fillets, cut into 3-cm (1¼-in) cubes

1 large red capsicum, cut into 3-cm (1¼-in) squares

tahini dip (page 31), to serve

You will need 12 × 20-cm (8-in) skewers: if using bamboo skewers, soak in water for at least 20 minutes before threading.

Remove zest (in strips) from 2 of the lemons, then juice them. In a large bowl combine the lemon zest and juice, oil, onion, bay leaves and oregano, and season with salt and pepper. Toss chicken in the marinade until all pieces are coated. Cover, and refrigerate for at least 2 hours (or overnight).

Heat a barbecue or grill to high. Cut remaining 2 lemons into wedges.

Remove meat from marinade, draining off any excess (reserve marinade). Thread onto skewers, alternating with onion and capsicum pieces, and including a bay leaf and a strip of lemon zest on each skewer.

Grill the skewers for 8–12 minutes, occasionally turning and basting with marinade, until golden-brown and meat is cooked through. Serve skewers with lemon wedges and tahini dip.

∾ This marinade is also delicious for lamb. Cut 1 kg (2 lb 3 oz) boned lamb leg into 2-cm (¾-in) pieces and proceed as above. Serve with yoghurt, lemon and mint sauce (page 246).

Meat

In the Middle East, meat was originally recognised as the food of the rich or was reserved for special occasions. Later, household cooks would add small amounts of meat to dishes of vegetables or grains, or to stuffings and pastries, to make the meat go further. Lamb and mutton were traditionally the meats of choice, but beef and veal are becoming more common: generally beef can be substituted for lamb in these recipes, and a mixture of lamb and beef used instead of lamb mince. Stuffed whole baby lamb or kid (once typically cooked in the local baker's wood-fired oven) is a festive speciality – the recipe for roast stuffed lamb leg is a scaled-down version.

Meat often receives slow, lengthy cooking: familiar examples include the stew-like sauces of Iran (called khoreshtha), and shawarma, shaved meat slow-roasted on a spit for many hours. Cubed meat or spiced mince (kofta kebab) is grilled on skewers, usually over coals.

< Kofta Kebabs (page 182)

Kofta Kebabs

Kofta meshwi

Makes 16

1 kg (2 lb 3 oz) lamb or beef
   mince

2 onions, finely chopped

2 teaspoons salt

freshly ground black pepper

1 cup finely chopped fresh
   flat-leaf parsley

2 teaspoons baharat (page 237)

olive oil, for brushing

warmed flatbread, to serve

tomato and cucumber salad
   with sumac (page 71), to
   serve

You will need 16 × 20-cm (8-in) skewers: if using bamboo skewers, soak them in water for at least 20 minutes before threading.

Preheat barbecue or grill to high.

Place half the meat, onions, salt, parsley and baharat in the bowl of a food processor. Add a generous grinding of pepper. Blend until well combined and paste-like. Transfer to a bowl, then repeat with the other half of the ingredients.

With wet hands, take a small handful of the meat mixture and mould it around a skewer into a sausage shape about 10 cm (4 in) long. Brush lightly with oil, then set aside while you prepare the remaining skewers. Cook kebabs on preheated grill for 4–5 minutes, turning frequently, until browned all over and cooked through.

Have ready warmed flatbread topped with tomatoes and cucumber salad. Serve kebabs on the bread, to catch the cooking juices. (Alternatively, serve the kofta with rice and salad.)

ରୁ You can use a mixture of lamb and beef if you like. Instead of the baharat, you could use 1 teaspoon each ground cumin and coriander, or 1 teaspoon ground allspice.

Grilled Butterflied Leg of Lamb

Serves 6–8

1 × 2.5-kg (5½-lb) leg of lamb, butterflied (ask your butcher to do this)

2 cloves garlic, cut into fine slivers

1 large onion, roughly chopped

⅓ cup (80 ml/3 fl oz) olive oil

zest and juice of 2 lemons

2 cups fresh flat-leaf parsley leaves

½ cup fresh mint leaves

1 tablespoon dried oregano or thyme

1 teaspoon salt

freshly ground black pepper

1 teaspoon ground paprika

1 teaspoon ground cinnamon

1 teaspoon ground cumin

1 teaspoon ground coriander

½ teaspoon ground allspice

Pierce meat all over with the tip of a sharp knife. Slide garlic slivers into the cuts and place meat in a large, shallow, ceramic or glass dish.

Place onion in the bowl of a food processor and blend to a liquidy paste. Pour into a small bowl, add the oil, lemon zest and juice, and stir to mix well. Add the fresh and dried herbs, salt, pepper and spices, and mix thoroughly. Pour mixture over lamb and rub all over to coat well, cover with cling wrap and marinate for 24 hours in the refrigerator.

Remove lamb from fridge an hour before cooking. Preheat barbecue to high, or oven to 200°C (390°F).

Remove lamb from the marinade (reserve marinade). Barbecue the lamb, or roast in preheated oven in a large baking dish, for 45–60 minutes for medium-rare, or until cooked to your liking. Turn lamb halfway through cooking time and baste with marinade. Rest meat, covered, for 15 minutes before carving.

Serve with flatbread, yoghurt and garlic sauce (see note page 246) and cucumber and fetta salad (page 62), or with tabbouleh (page 70) and tahini sauce (see note page 31).

Grilled Lamb Chops

Serves 4–6

3 tablespoons (60 ml/2 fl oz)
olive oil

1 clove garlic, crushed with
½ teaspoon sea salt

zest of 1 lemon

½ teaspoon finely crushed
coriander seeds

¼ teaspoon finely crushed
black peppercorns

½ teaspoon baharat (page 237)

8 lamb chump chops or
12 lamb cutlets

1 red onion, cut into 6 wedges
and layers separated

In a large shallow dish combine the oil, garlic, lemon zest and spices. Add the chops and turn to coat all over with the marinade. Cover with plastic wrap and refrigerate for a minimum of 2 hours (or overnight).

Remove the dish from the fridge half an hour before cooking. Preheat the barbecue or grill to high.

Place the onions and chops on the barbecue or grill. Cook the chops for 3 minutes on each side, or until cooked to your liking. Cook onions (toss regularly so they cook evenly) until golden-brown around edges and softened.

Serve with flatbread and a green salad, or tabbouleh (page 70).

Lamb Tartare with Burghul

Kibbeh nayeh

Serves 6

⅓ cup (60 g/2 oz) coarse burghul (cracked wheat)

1 cup (250 ml/8½ fl oz) hot water

225 g (8 oz) lamb fillet, trimmed of sinew and diced

2 shallots, finely chopped

1 teaspoon ground sweet paprika

¼ teaspoon ground cayenne

½ teaspoon ground cumin

2 teaspoons sumac

1 tablespoon chopped fresh flat-leaf parsley

½ teaspoon sea salt

freshly ground black pepper

olive oil, to serve

1 cup fresh mint leaves

1 cup fresh coriander leaves

lettuce leaves or flatbread, to serve

pickled turnips (page 236), to serve

2 lemons, cut into wedges

Soak burghul in the hot water for 10 minutes. Drain, place in a clean tea towel and squeeze out excess moisture. Put burghul in a large ceramic or glass bowl and refrigerate until chilled.

Pulse the meat in a food processor until finely chopped and paste-like. Add meat to the chilled burghul and combine well. Add the shallots, spices, parsley, salt and a generous grinding of pepper. Knead for 5 minutes to form a smooth paste.

Spread the meat mixture onto a flat plate. Cover with cling wrap and chill in the refrigerator for 1 hour. (You can prepare the dish to this point up to 6 hours ahead.)

When ready to serve, drizzle the surface of the kibbeh with olive oil and scatter with the herbs. To eat, roll portions of the meat mixture and the herbs in lettuce leaves, or bread if preferred. Serve with pickled turnips and lemon wedges alongside.

ଉ You can substitute beef fillet for the lamb. The meat must be of the best quality as it is eaten raw – do not use pre-minced meat. You can use the finely grated zest and juice of ½ lemon instead of sumac.

Veal-shank Stew with Moghrabieh, Tomatoes & Herbs

Serves 4

3 tablespoons (60 ml/2 fl oz) olive oil

4 veal (or lamb) shanks, French-trimmed

1 onion, finely chopped

1 × 400-g (14-oz) can chopped tomatoes

2 carrots, diced

1 tablespoon tomato paste

½ teaspoon ground cumin

½ teaspoon ground paprika

¼ teaspoon ground turmeric

pinch of ground cayenne

1 cinnamon stick

1 teaspoon salt

freshly ground black pepper

1.5 L (3 pt 3 fl oz) chicken stock

⅔ cup moghrabieh (giant couscous)

¼ cup chopped fresh coriander

¼ cup chopped fresh flat-leaf parsley

¼ cup chopped fresh mint

juice of 1 lemon

Heat half the oil in a heavy-based frying pan over medium–high heat. Add shanks and cook for 5 minutes, turning to brown all over. Set aside.

Heat remaining oil in a large saucepan over medium heat. Add the onion and cook for 5 minutes until softened. Add the browned veal shanks, tomatoes, carrots, tomato paste, spices, salt, pepper and stock, then simmer gently for 15 minutes (skim off any scum that rises to the surface). Cover and cook for a further 45 minutes. >

Stir the moghrabieh into the stew and simmer, uncovered, for 30 minutes or until the veal is tender and cooked through. Stir in the fresh herbs and lemon juice, and cook for another 5 minutes. Adjust seasoning, if needed.

Serve immediately.

Lamb Cooked in a Yoghurt Sauce

Serves 6–8

2 onions, each cut into
   6 wedges

2 tablespoons (40 ml/1½ fl oz)
   olive oil

2 teaspoon baharat (page 237)

4 cloves garlic, crushed with
   1 teaspoon salt

1 teaspoon ground turmeric

1.5–2 kg (3 lb 5 oz–4 lb 6 oz)
   lamb shoulder or leg in one
   piece, trimmed of excess fat

2 cups (500 ml/17 fl oz)
   stabilised yoghurt (see
   page 9)

1 cinnamon stick

⅓ cup toasted pine nuts

Preheat the oven to 190°C (375°F). Place onion wedges in a heavy-based casserole dish (cast iron is ideal) large enough to hold the lamb.

Combine the oil with the baharat, garlic and turmeric. Using a small sharp knife, pierce the lamb in several places and then rub the oil paste all over. Sit lamb on top of onions in the casserole and cover with lid. Roast for 20 minutes, then turn meat over, replace lid and roast for another 20 minutes.

Remove casserole from oven and spread the yoghurt over the meat to cover, basting with any cooking juices from the dish. Add the cinnamon stick, return to the oven and cook (uncovered) for 1 hour or until meat is tender. Transfer to a platter and sprinkle with pine nuts before serving.

℧ Traditionally this dish would be served with plain rice and flatbread.

Beef & Vegetable Stew

Khoresh

Serves 4

2 eggplants, cut into 2-cm
(¾-in) cubes

salt

½ cup (125 ml/4 fl oz) olive oil

1 onion, diced

450 g (1 lb) stewing beef
(gravy beef, oyster blade),
cubed

½ teaspoon ground ginger

1 teaspoon ground cinnamon

½ teaspoon ground allspice

¼ teaspoon freshly grated
nutmeg

½ teaspoon ground turmeric

4 tomatoes, peeled and
chopped

1 tablespoon tomato paste

⅓ cup yellow split peas or
brown lentils

1 loomi (dried lime), or the
juice and finely grated zest
of ½ lemon

1 cup pitted fresh morello
cherries

Iranian steamed rice (page 75),
to serve

Place eggplant cubes in a colander and sprinkle with salt. Set aside for 30 minutes, then rinse under running water and drain well. Pat dry with paper towels.

Heat one-third of the oil in a large heavy-based saucepan over medium heat. Add the eggplant and cook for 5 minutes or until golden. Remove with a slotted spoon and set aside.

Add another third of the oil to the pan and cook onion for 8–10 minutes, until softened and lightly golden. Remove from pan, and add to the eggplant.

Increase heat to high and add remaining oil to pan. Stir in the meat in two or three batches and cook until browned all over. Reduce heat to medium, return the eggplant and onion to the saucepan, add the spices and stir for 1 minute. Add tomatoes, tomato paste, split peas or lentils, lime (or lemon zest and juice), and enough water to just cover. Put lid on saucepan, bring to the boil, then reduce heat and simmer gently for 1½ hours.

After this time, stir in the cherries and cook for a further 20 minutes or until meat is very tender. Adjust seasoning with salt and taste for sweet–sour balance, adding a little sugar or lemon juice if necessary. Serve with chelou.

80 There are many versions of this stew-like sauce, which tends to include whatever fruit and vegetables are in season. You can use fresh pomegranate seeds, dried sour cherries or dried prunes when morello cherries are not in season. The eggplants can be replaced with 4 zucchini (no need to salt them).

Persian Stuffed Meat Rolls

Serves 4

450 g (1 lb) lean lamb mince

1½ cups cooked short-grain rice

2 cloves garlic, chopped

1½ teaspoons baharat (page 237)

1 teaspoon salt

olive oil or vegetable oil for frying

SPLIT PEA FILLING

⅓ cup yellow split peas

1 tablespoon samneh

1 onion, finely chopped

¼ teaspoon ground cardamom

½ teaspoon baharat (page 237)

2 tablespoons chopped fresh flat-leaf parsley

salt and freshly ground black pepper

To make the filling, place split peas in a saucepan and cover with water. Bring to the boil, then reduce heat and simmer for 30 minutes or until soft. Drain well.

Next, melt the samneh in a frying pan over a medium heat. Add the onion and sauté for 10 minutes until softened and lightly coloured. Stir in the spices, parsley and drained split peas, season to taste with salt and pepper, remove from heat and set aside. >

To make the meat rolls, place the lamb, rice, garlic, baharat and salt in the bowl of a food processor. Blend until well combined and paste-like. With wet hands, take a golfball-sized portion of the meat mixture and shape into a ball. Press a hole in the centre with your thumb, forming the rim into a shell about 5 mm (¼ in) thick. Fill the centre with a teaspoonful of the prepared filling, seal the opening and mould into an egg shape. Repeat process with the remaining mixture. (You can prepare the rolls to this stage up to a day ahead: keep covered in the refrigerator until ready to cook.)

Heat oil to a depth of 1.5 cm (⅝ in) in a frying pan over medium–high heat. Cook rolls, in batches, for about 8–10 minutes (turn them halfway through cooking time), until golden-brown all over and meat is cooked through. Drain on paper towels.

Serve immediately.

๛ You can serve these rolls as a meze or, with a salad and warmed flatbread, as a main meal.

Pot-roasted Veal Shanks with Potatoes

Serves 6

3 tablespoons (60 ml/ 2 fl oz) olive oil

6 French-trimmed veal shanks

⅓ cup (80 ml/3 fl oz) freshly squeezed lemon juice

2 teaspoons dried oregano

1 teaspoon ground turmeric

2 cloves garlic, cut into slivers

salt and freshly ground black pepper

700 g (1 lb 9 oz) small kipfler potatoes, tossed in about 2 tablespoons olive oil

Preheat the oven to 160°C (320°F).

Heat oil to medium–hot in a heavy-based casserole pot large enough to hold all the shanks comfortably. Cook shanks in two batches until browned all over.

Return all the shanks to the pot, add the lemon juice, oregano, turmeric, garlic, salt and pepper, tossing to coat meat well. Cover with a tight-fitting lid and bake in preheated oven for 1 hour. Remove from oven, turn meat over and stir in the potatoes, then bake for a further 1–1½ hours until potatoes are cooked through and meat is very tender.

Serve shanks and potatoes with pot juices poured over.

🔊 You can substitute lamb shanks for the veal (remove any excess fat before cooking).

Meatballs in Tomato Sauce

Serves 4–6

MEATBALLS

450 g (½ lb) beef mince

450 g (½ lb) lamb mince

1 onion, finely chopped

1 teaspoon ground cumin

1 slice white bread

1 teaspoon salt

freshly ground black pepper

1 cup roughly chopped coriander

1 cup roughly chopped flat-leaf parsley

½ cup chopped walnuts

TOMATO SAUCE

700 g (1 lb 9 oz) tomatoes, peeled and chopped, or 800 g (1 lb 12 oz) canned chopped tomatoes

½ teaspoon ground cumin

½ teaspoon ground cardamom

1 cup chopped flat-leaf parsley

¼ teaspoon ground cayenne pepper (optional)

To prepare the meatballs, place all the ingredients except the walnuts in the bowl of a food processor. Blend until well combined, stopping machine and scraping down sides occasionally, until mixture is paste-like. Add the walnuts and pulse until just combined. With wet hands, shape the meat mixture into walnut-sized balls and set aside while you make the sauce.

Place all sauce ingredients in a large saucepan and set over a high heat. Add 2 cups (500 ml/17 fl oz) water, bring to the boil and then reduce to a simmer. Place meatballs gently in the simmering sauce, adding extra water if necessary to cover. Put on lid and simmer for 30 minutes, then remove lid and simmer for a further 30 minutes until meatballs are cooked and the sauce is reduced and thick.

Serve with rice.

Roast Stuffed Lamb Leg

Serves 6–8

⅓ cup raisins

½ quantity saffron rice with nuts (page 76)

2.5-kg (5½-lb) leg of lamb, tunnel-boned (ask your butcher to do this)

3 cloves garlic, cut into slivers

½ teaspoon black peppercorns

1 teaspoon coriander seeds

1 teaspoon ground ginger

1 teaspoon salt

2 tablespoons (40 ml/1½ fl oz) olive oil

Preheat the oven to 220°C (420°F).

First, prepare the stuffing by stirring the raisins through the cooked rice. Fill the lamb cavity with this mixture (there may be some stuffing left over) and seal the open ends with small metal skewers. Pierce lamb all over with the point of a sharp knife and insert garlic slivers.

In a mortar, grind the peppercorns and coriander to a fine powder. Combine all the spices with the salt and oil, and rub over the lamb to coat evenly. Transfer to a roasting dish and place in preheated oven, then reduce temperature to 160°C (320°F) and cook for 2½ hours, basting occasionally, until meat is cooked all the way through. Serve with salads and rice.

෨ If desired, make the full quantity of saffron rice and serve the extra as an accompaniment.

Sweets & Drinks

Sweets are always on offer in Middle Eastern homes; another expression of the people's liberal hospitality. Sweet treats can be as simple as a platter of fresh seasonal fruit (perhaps perfumed with rosewater syrup or scattered with nuts) or as intricate as spiced, honey-fragrant pastries filled with nuts or dried fruit. The best-known sweet pastry, baklava, is easy to prepare at home and is great to share on any occasion.

Making, serving and drinking coffee is surrounded with ceremony, tradition and etiquette. Coffee is always offered, invariably along with a plate of sweet nibbles, when discussing business or when visitors arrive at home. Spices are often used to aromatise and flavour both coffee and tea. Sweet drinks (known as sherbets) are made from sugar syrups flavoured with various fruits: although you can buy prepared syrup, it is easy to make your own, so do try the recipes in this section.

< Easter Cakes (page 206)

Easter Cakes

Ma'amoul

Makes about 30

icing sugar, for dusting

DATE FILLING

450 g (1 lb) fresh dates, stones removed

3 tablespoons (60 ml/2 fl oz) freshly squeezed orange juice

1 tablespoon (20 ml/¾ fl oz) orange-blossom water

SEMOLINA DOUGH

1½ cups (180 g/6½ oz) fine semolina

1½ cups (225 g/½ lb) plain flour

250 g (9 oz) unsalted butter, cut into cubes

2 tablespoons (40 ml/1½ fl oz) orange-blossom water

3–4 tablespoons (60–80 ml/ 2–3 fl oz) milk

To make the filling, place dates and orange juice in a saucepan over medium heat. Stir until the dates break down into a thick paste (about 5 minutes). Remove from heat and set aside to cool, then stir in the orange-blossom water.

To make the dough, place the semolina, flour and butter in the bowl of a food processor and blend until mixture resembles coarse breadcrumbs. Pour in the orange-blossom water and enough milk to make a soft dough. Remove dough and knead for a minute on a lightly floured surface until smooth. Cover with plastic wrap and refrigerate for 30 minutes.

Preheat the oven to 160°C (230°F). Line two baking trays with baking paper.

Take walnut-sized pieces of dough and shape into balls. Use your thumb to make a hollow in the centre of each ball, forming a pot shape. Fill the hollow with a teaspoonful of date mixture, then seal over and mould back into a ball.

Place balls on prepared baking trays. Decorate the tops by pressing with the tines of a fork or the tip of a spoon (this creates pockets in the cakes that will capture the icing sugar). Bake in preheated oven for 20–25 minutes until cakes are lightly coloured. Leave to cool on trays for 10 minutes (the cakes will harden), then transfer to a wire rack to cool completely.

Dust a baking tray generously with icing sugar. Transfer cakes to the tray, then dust tops with more icing sugar to coat all over. Store in an airtight container.

- If there is any leftover filling, it will keep (in an airtight container) in the refrigerator for 1 month.
- You can use a walnut filling instead of the date filling: combine 185 g (6½ oz) finely chopped walnuts with ¼ cup (60 g/2 oz) caster sugar, 1 tablespoon (20 ml/¾ fl oz) orange-blossom water and ½ teaspoon ground nutmeg.

Nut & Sesame Seed Candy

Makes about 30

½ cup (150 g/5 oz) honey

1½ cups (345 g/12 oz) caster sugar

1½ cups sesame seeds

½ cup chopped pistachios

Brush an 18-cm × 28-cm (7-in × 11-in) slice tin with olive oil.

Heat honey and sugar in a heavy-based saucepan over low heat until sugar dissolves. Increase heat to medium and cook, watching carefully, for about 10–15 minutes or until syrup reaches soft-ball stage (to test, drop a little syrup into cold water: it should form a soft, squeezable ball) or 115°C (265°F) on a sugar thermometer.

Working quickly, stir in the sesame seeds and pistachios and continue cooking, without any further stirring, until the syrup reaches hard-ball stage or 130°C (265°F) on a sugar thermometer. The sesame seeds will cook in the syrup and turn golden-brown. Pour immediately into prepared tin and use an oiled spatula to spread it evenly. Set aside until cool enough to touch.

Turn candy out onto a board and cut into bite-sized diamonds or other shapes. Leave to cool completely, then wrap individually in baking paper or cellophane.

Almond Shortbread Rings

Ghrayebah

Makes about 35

2½ cups (375 g/13 oz) plain flour

½ teaspoon ground cardamom

250 g (9 oz) softened unsalted butter

1 cup (160 g/6 oz) pure icing sugar

about 35 blanched almonds

Preheat the oven to 160°C (320°F). Line two baking trays with baking paper.

Sift flour and cardamom together into a small bowl. With an electric mixer, beat butter and sifted sugar until creamy and pale. Gradually stir in the flour until it is all incorporated. Knead until the dough is soft and does not stick to your hands, adding a little extra flour if necessary.

Take walnut-sized pieces of dough and roll each into a sausage about 10 cm (4 in) long. Bring the ends together to form a ring, place a blanched almond over the join, then transfer rings to prepared trays, leaving space for spreading. Bake in preheated oven for 20–25 minutes or until the almond is light golden (the biscuit should not colour). Leave to cool on the trays.

Store in an airtight container and serve with coffee or tea.

℘ These are fragile biscuits, so handle them with care. They can be decorated with pine nuts or chopped pistachios instead of almonds.

Shredded Pastry Filled with Sweetened Cheese

Makes 8

500 g (1 lb 2 oz) fresh ricotta cheese

1 teaspoon ground cinnamon

finely grated zest of 1 lemon

1 tablespoon (20 ml/¾ fl oz) warmed honey

250 g (9 oz) kataifi pastry

⅔ cup (160 ml/5½ fl oz) melted butter

1 quantity orange-blossom syrup (see note page 229), chilled

½ cup chopped walnuts

Place ricotta, cinnamon, lemon zest and honey in a bowl and mix until smooth and well combined.

Preheat the oven to 175°C (350°F). Brush eight 125-ml (4-fl oz) ramekins with butter.

Unravel pastry and loosen strands by pulling gently with your fingers. Place in a large bowl, pour melted butter over and then toss until pastry strands are evenly coated. Using half the pastry, line the bases of the ramekins and press down to compact the strands. Spread ricotta mixture over the pastry, then top with remaining pastry and press down again to flatten the surface.

Place ramekins on a baking tray and bake for 35–45 minutes, until pastry is golden-brown. Remove from oven and immediately pour the cold syrup over. When cool, invert pastries onto a plate and serve sprinkled with walnuts.

Baklava

Makes about 30

seeds from 3 cardamom pods

2½ cups ground almonds or pistachios

1 cup chopped blanched almonds

½ cup (110 g/4 oz) caster sugar

10 sheets filo pastry

¾ cup (180 ml/6 fl oz) melted unsalted butter

ROSEWATER & CARDAMOM SYRUP

seeds from 2 cardamom pods

1 quantity rosewater syrup (page 229)

For the syrup, crush the cardamom seeds finely in a mortar. Add to the prepared rosewater syrup and boil it for a further 10 minutes or until it thickens enough to coat the back of a spoon. Cool, then refrigerate until required.

Preheat the oven to 160°C (320°F). Brush the base and sides of a deep 25-cm × 30-cm (10-in × 12-in) baking dish with melted butter.

To assemble the baklava, finely crush the cardamom seeds in a mortar and combine in a bowl with the nuts and sugar. Brush three sheets of filo with melted butter, place on top of each other and use to line the base and sides of the baking dish. (Cover the unused filo sheets with a damp tea towel as you work.) Scatter one-third of the nut mixture over the pastry and cover with another two filo sheets which you have brushed with butter. >

Repeat these layers twice more, ending with the last three sheets of filo, each brushed with melted butter.

Trim pastry edges around the top of the dish with a sharp knife. Carefully cut even-sized diamond shapes all the way through to the base of the dish. Bake in preheated oven for 40 minutes, then increase heat to 190°C (375°F) and bake for a further 15–20 minutes until pastry is light-golden and puffed. Pour the cold syrup evenly over the baklava while it is still hot and then leave to cool. Leave for at least 2 hours before slicing into diamonds.

ဢ Baklava can be stored in an airtight container in a cool place for 4 days (do not refrigerate), though the pastry will gradually lose its crispness.

Watermelon with Summer Berries

Serves 6

1.5 kg (3 lb 5 oz) watermelon

150 g (5 oz) raspberries

150 g (5 oz) strawberries

¼ cup pistachios, for garnish

rose petals (optional), for garnish

clotted cream (page 245), to serve

SPICED ROSEWATER SYRUP

½ cup (110 g/4 oz) caster sugar

1 cinnamon stick

3 cardamom pods, split

1 tablespoon (20 ml/¾ fl oz) lemon juice

1 cup fresh mint leaves

2 teaspoons rosewater

First make the syrup. Place sugar and ½ cup (125 ml/4 fl oz) water in a saucepan over medium heat and stir until sugar dissolves. Bring to the boil, reduce heat to low and add the cinnamon, cardamom, lemon juice and mint leaves. Simmer for 10–15 minutes or until the syrup thickens and coats the back of a spoon. Remove from heat and stir in the rosewater. Set aside to cool, then pass syrup through a strainer and discard solids. Keep in an airtight container in the refrigerator for up to 1 week.

Remove rind from the watermelon and cut the flesh into small triangles. Place melon and berries in a bowl, pour the chilled syrup over and toss gently to combine. Spoon onto a platter or into individual bowls and scatter with pistachios and rose petals (if using). Serve with a dollop of cream.

Rice & Almond Pudding

Muhallabia

Serves 6

½ cup (75 g/2½ oz) ground rice

3 cups (750 ml/25 fl oz) milk

¼ cup (60 g/2 oz) caster sugar

¼ teaspoon ground cardamom (optional)

1 tablespoon (20 ml/¾ fl oz) rosewater or orange-blossom water

½ cup (60 g/2 oz) ground almonds

2 tablespoons chopped pistachios, for garnish

¼ cup fresh orange cordial (page 230) (optional)

fresh pomegranate seets (when in season), for garnish

In a small bowl stir together the ground rice and ½ cup (125 ml/4 fl oz) of the milk to form a smooth paste.

Place remaining milk in a saucepan and bring just to the boil. Reduce heat to low–medium, add the sugar, cardamom (if using) and prepared rice paste, stirring constantly with a whisk to prevent lumps, until mixture thickens and coats the back of a spoon. (Bubbles will appear, but if milk starts to catch on the base reduce heat to low.) Stir in the rosewater and cook for 2 minutes. Remove pan from heat, stir in almonds and leave to cool for 10 minutes. Spoon into individual glass dishes, cover with cling wrap to prevent a skin forming and refrigerate for 2 hours until chilled.

To serve, sprinkle with pistachios, and drizzle with a little orange cordial, if using. Garnish with pomegranate seeds when available.

Pancakes with Sweet Nuts & Orange Blossom

Ataif

Serves 6–8

2 teaspoons (7 g/¼ oz) dried yeast

1 teaspoon sugar

1½ cups (375 ml/12½ fl oz) lukewarm water

1½ cups (225 g/8 oz) plain flour

olive oil or samneh for frying

clotted cream (page 245) or double cream, to serve

orange-blossom syrup (see note page 229), to serve

SWEET NUT FILLING

1½ cups chopped pistachios or walnuts

2 tablespoons (30 g/1 oz) soft brown sugar

¼ teaspoon freshly grated nutmeg

½ teaspoon ground cardamom or cinnamon

In a small bowl dissolve the yeast and sugar in one-third of the lukewarm water. Set aside for 10 minutes or until the surface is covered in bubbles.

Sift the flour into a large bowl and make a well in the centre. Pour in the yeast mixture and remaining warm water, and gradually stir in flour with a whisk until all is incorporated and the batter is smooth. Cover the bowl with a clean cloth or cling wrap and leave in a warm place for about 1 hour, until the batter has risen and the surface is bubbly.

Meanwhile, combine all the filling ingredients in a bowl. >

Heat a large non-stick frying pan over medium heat, then grease the base with a film of oil or samneh. Ladle in about 2 tablespoons of batter, to form a 10-cm (4-in) round. When the surface of the pancake is covered in bubbles and the base is golden, turn to cook the other side. Repeat until all the batter has been used, stacking the cooked pancakes on a plate as you go and keeping them warm.

To serve, place one pancake on a plate and sprinkle with some nut filling, then top with another pancake. Add a dollop of cream, and sprinkle with a little extra nut filling to garnish. Drizzle syrup over and serve immediately.

&ᴑ These Arabic pancakes are thicker and fluffier than French-style ones and make a delicious weekend breakfast treat. If preferred, warm the orange-blossom syrup gently before adding.

Rice Pudding

Serves 6

⅔ cup short-grain rice, washed (see page 13)

1 L (34 fl oz) milk

2 tablespoons (40 ml/1½ fl oz) honey

½ cup (110 g/4 oz) caster sugar

1 tablespoon (20 ml/¾ fl oz) orange-blossom water

dried fruit compote (page 224), to serve

¼ cup chopped pistachios or walnuts, for garnish

Place rice and 2 cups (500 ml/17 fl oz) water in a saucepan over medium heat and bring to the boil. Reduce heat and simmer for about 15 minutes, stirring occasionally to prevent sticking, until rice is cooked and the water absorbed.

Stir the milk, honey and sugar into the rice and bring to a simmer. Cook for 30 minutes until mixture is thick, stirring from time to time to prevent sticking. Stir in the orange-blossom water and serve warm, topped with the fruit compote and sprinkled with the nuts.

Dried Fruit Compote

Serves 4–6

1 cup dried apricots

1 cup pitted prunes

1½ cups dried figs

1 cinnamon stick

2 cardamom pods, split

3 cloves

1 strip lemon zest

1 cup (220 g/8 oz) caster sugar

chopped walnuts or pistachios,
   for garnish (optional)

cream or yoghurt, to serve

Place dried fruit and about 1 litre (34 fl oz) water in a saucepan and set aside for an hour. Then stir in the spices, lemon zest and sugar until sugar has dissolved.

Place pan over a medium heat and slowly bring to the boil. Reduce heat and simmer for 15 minutes, or until syrup is thick and the mixture jam-like (the fruit should be soft but not mushy). Transfer to a bowl to cool, then cover and refrigerate until needed.

Serve sprinkled with nuts if desired, and with a jug of cream or yoghurt alongside for pouring.

∞ The compote will keep, refrigerated, for about 5 days.

Arabic Coffee

Makes 4 small cups

1½ tablespoons freshly
   ground Turkish coffee

1 cardamom pod

2 teaspoons caster sugar

Place the coffee in a small saucepan with 1 cup (250 ml/8½ fl oz) water, the cardamom and the sugar. Bring to the boil over a medium–high heat, then remove from heat as soon as the froth rises. Stir, then return to the heat and bring to the boil again, once again removing from heat when the froth rises. Let the froth settle, then repeat the process once more. Pour immediately into small cups and let stand for a moment before drinking so the grounds settle to the bottom.

∞ In the Middle East, coffee is prepared in a long-handled copper or brass pot known as a rakweh, though a small saucepan will do. The coffee is very finely ground, almost powder-like.

Fresh Lemonade

Makes about 1 L (34 fl oz)

1 cup (220 g/8 oz) caster sugar

1 cup (250 ml/8½ fl oz) freshly squeezed lemon juice

finely grated zest of 2 lemons

orange-blossom water, to taste

Place sugar and 1 litre (34 fl oz) water in a large bowl and stir to dissolve sugar. Add the lemon juice and zest, and stir to combine. Cover and refrigerate for 4 hours to allow flavours to infuse, then strain into a jug, adding orange-blossom water to taste.

Serve over crushed ice.

- You can use rosewater instead of the orange-blossom water.
- The lemonade will keep for 3 days in the refrigerator.

Rosewater Syrup

Makes about 500 ml (17 fl oz)

450 g (1 lb) caster sugar

1 tablespoon (20 ml/¾ fl oz) freshly squeezed lemon juice, strained

⅓ cup (80 ml/3 oz) rosewater

Place sugar and 1 cup (250 ml/8 ½ fl oz) water in a saucepan and stir over medium heat until sugar is dissolved. Bring to the boil, add lemon juice, then reduce heat and simmer (without stirring) for 10 minutes or until the consistency of thin honey. Add the rosewater and simmer for a further 2 minutes. Remove from the heat and leave to cool.

Pour syrup into a clean sterilised bottle and seal.

To serve as a cordial, pour 2–3 tablespoons over crushed ice and fill glass with chilled water or soda water. This syrup may also be used in desserts like baklava (page 215).

⁊ Rosewater syrup will keep in the refrigerator for a month.

⁊ To make orange-blossom syrup, substitute 3 tablespoons (60 ml/2 fl oz) orange-blossom water for the rosewater.

Fresh Orange Cordial

Makes about 750 ml (25 fl oz)

**475 ml (1 pt) freshly squeezed
orange juice (about
10 oranges)**

500 g (1 lb 2 oz) caster sugar

**1 tablespoon (20 ml/¾ fl oz)
freshly squeezed lemon juice**

Place the orange juice and sugar in a saucepan and stir over a medium heat until the sugar is dissolved. Bring to the boil, add lemon juice, reduce heat and then simmer for 10 minutes without stirring. Remove from the heat and cool. Pour into clean sterilised bottles and seal.

To serve, add 2–3 tablespoons cordial to a glass filled with crushed ice, and pour in chilled water, sparkling water or soda water.

ℰ The cordial will keep in the refrigerator for a month.

Yoghurt Drink

Serves 6

2 cups (500 ml/17 fl oz) Greek-
  style yoghurt

about 1 cup (250 ml/8½ fl oz)
  chilled water

1 tablespoon fresh mint leaves
  (optional)

salt

Place yoghurt and water in a blender and blend until smooth. If using mint, add to blended yoghurt and process until finely chopped. Season to taste with a little salt.

Serve chilled, over crushed ice if desired.

Strawberry Water Ice

Serves 6

1 cup (220 g/8 oz) caster sugar

1 tablespoon (20 ml/¾ fl oz)
freshly squeezed lemon juice

600 g (1 lb 5 oz) strawberries,
leaves removed

1 tablespoon finely chopped
fresh mint

3 tablespoons (60 ml/2 fl oz)
milk

Place sugar and 2 cups (500 ml/17 fl oz) water in a heavy-based saucepan over medium heat and stir to dissolve. Add the lemon juice and bring to the boil, cook for 5 minutes, then pour into a large bowl and set aside to cool.

Place strawberries and mint in a blender and blend to a purée. Combine with the cooled syrup, add milk and stir to mix well. Pour mixture into a shallow metal tray (a lamington tin is ideal), freeze for 1 hour, then remove from freezer and break up any frozen pieces with a fork. Repeat this step four times every hour, running a fork through the ice as it sets.

Spoon into serving glasses and serve immediately.

Extras

The Middle Eastern table always includes a range of dressings, pickles, sauces and other condiments to accompany the main dishes, adding flavour and contrast to a meal. Spice mixes such as fragrant salt, baharat (the Arabic word for 'spice') and za'atar, as well as flavoured oils, are used to season many dishes before cooking and are also commonly sprinkled over food once it's served.

Yoghurt appears in many guises, including a variety of sauces for meats and vegetables. Tarator, a traditional nut sauce of which there are variations in many parts of the world, is also served with all manner of dishes. Syrups and preserves perfumed with fruits and flowers date back many centuries in Iran and other Arab countries.

‹ Pickled Turnips (page 236)

Pickled Turnips

900 g (2 lb) baby or small turnips, peeled and quartered

¼ cup celery leaves

6 black peppercorns

2 cloves garlic, peeled

1 small beetroot, peeled and quartered

300 ml (10fl oz) white-wine vinegar

⅓ cup (65 g/2¼ oz) sea salt

Pack turnip pieces into a warm sterilised 2-litre (4 pt 4-fl oz) jar, with the celery leaves, peppercorns, garlic and beetroot scattered in between.

Bring 950 ml (2 pt) water and the vinegar to the boil in a stainless steel saucepan over high heat. Stir in the salt until dissolved and pour mixture over the vegetables to cover well, shaking the jar to release any trapped air bubbles. Leave to cool, then seal the jar.

Store in a cool dark place. The pickle will be ready to eat in 7 days and should be opened within a month (refrigerate after opening and use within 2 weeks).

∞ Pickled cauliflower can be made in the same way. Instead of the turnips, use a head of cauliflower, divided into florets. Omit the peppercorns, garlic and beetroot, and add a sprig of dill and 1 long fresh red chilli.

Baharat

3 tablespoons black peppercorns, finely ground

1½ tablespoons finely ground coriander seeds

2 tablespoons finely ground cumin seeds

2 teaspoons finely ground cardamom seeds

1 tablespoon ground cinnamon

1 tablespoon ground cloves

½ teaspoon freshly grated nutmeg

3 tablespoons ground sweet paprika

Combine all the ingredients and mix well. Store in an airtight jar in a cool dark place. Use within 3 months, though the flavour is fresher the sooner baharat is used.

∞ The combination of spices used for baharat is similar from household to household, but the proportions often vary.

∞ It is preferable to make this mix with freshly ground spices, rather than bought ground spices – the flavour will be far superior.

Yoghurt Cheese

Labne

Makes about 1 cup

½ teaspoon salt

3 cups (750 g/1 lb 10 oz) full-
fat Greek-style yoghurt

extra-virgin olive oil, to drizzle

Place a non-metal sieve over a bowl and line it with a large piece of muslin (or a new open-weave kitchen wipe) folded in half. Stir the salt through the yoghurt, then place the yoghurt in the centre of the cloth and fold over the corners to cover. Refrigerate and allow to drain for 12 hours, or overnight.

Transfer drained yoghurt to a bowl. Drizzle with olive oil and serve with olives and warmed flatbread.

⁊ To vary the flavour, stir a crushed clove of garlic through the yoghurt before draining, or serve the labne sprinkled with za'atar (page 244) or ground paprika.

⁊ To make labne balls, drain the yoghurt for 48 hours: the result should be a firm cheese. Roll heaped teaspoonfuls of the cheese into balls, with oiled hands. Place in a sterilised jar and cover with olive oil. Seal, and store in the refrigerator for up to 2 weeks. (For herbed labne balls, see page 25.)

Fragrant Salt

Makes about ½ cup

3 tablespoons sea salt
2 teaspoons cumin seeds
2 teaspoons coriander seeds
2 teaspoons fennel seeds

Crush each spice separately in a mortar until coarsely ground. Combine the salt and spices, store in a screw-top jar and use within 1 month.

∾ This salt may be sprinkled over spiced green olives (page 36), tomato and cucumber salad with sumac (page 71), fried little fish (page 150) or labne balls (see note page 238).

Rose Petal Jam

Makes 1 large jar

**4 cups freshly picked, deep-red
heavily scented rose petals**
2 cups (450 g/1 lb) caster sugar
juice of 2 lemons

Trim off the whitish base of each petal and discard. Rinse petals in a bowl of cold water and drain well in a colander.

Place drained petals in a large glass or ceramic bowl. Sprinkle with half the sugar and toss gently. Cover bowl with a clean tea towel and leave overnight (the sugar will draw out the scent and darken the petals).

Place the lemon juice, 2 cups (500 ml/17 fl oz) water and the remaining sugar in a large heavy-based saucepan over medium heat and stir until sugar dissolves. Bring to the boil and cook for 5 minutes, then remove from heat and stir in the rose petals and their syrup. Replace saucepan over medium heat, bring to a simmer and cook gently for 15 minutes or until the syrup is thick. Ladle into warm sterilised jars and set aside to cool. Seal with lids.

This jam is delicious served with pancakes (page 221) and clotted cream (page 245).

&) Do not use petals from plants that have been sprayed with pesticides.

Paprika Oil

Makes about ½ cup

**½ cup (125 ml/4 fl oz)
extra-virgin olive oil**

**2 teaspoons ground sweet
paprika**

1 clove garlic, chopped

Place all the ingredients in a small saucepan over a low–medium heat. When small bubbles begin to appear around the garlic, remove pan from heat. Set aside to cool completely, then pour oil through a muslin-lined sieve into a jar. Seal and store in a cool dark place.

- The oil is best used within 2 weeks.
- Drizzle over dishes such as lamb, tomato and pine-nut pizza (page 107), spiced pumpkin and tomato soup (page 48), or fried potatoes.

Nut Sauce

Tarator

Makes about 2 cups

1 cup chopped walnuts or
   hazelnuts, skins removed

1 cup fresh breadcrumbs

2 cloves garlic, chopped

about 200 ml (7 fl oz) olive oil

¼ cup white-wine vinegar

salt and freshly ground black
   pepper

Place nuts in the bowl of a food processor and blend until finely ground. Add breadcrumbs, 1 tablespoon (20 ml/¾ fl oz) water and the garlic, and blend again until well mixed. With the motor still running, add the oil slowly and gradually until all is incorporated. Pour in vinegar and blend until smooth, then season to taste with salt and pepper.

Serve with cooked vegetables such as fried eggplant (page 135).

∞ To make pine-nut tarator, replace the walnuts or hazelnuts with pine nuts and use lemon juice instead of vinegar. Serve with fish.

Za'atar

Makes about ½ cup

3 tablespoons sesame seeds

3 tablespoons dried thyme

1 heaped tablespoon ground sumac

salt

Put the sesame seeds into a frying pan over high heat and dry-fry them for a few minutes, shaking the pan occasionally, until toasted (watch carefully as they can burn). Tip into a small bowl and allow to cool.

Add thyme and sumac to the cooled sesame seeds, add a small pinch of salt and mix well.

Store in an airtight jar in a cool place, or in the refrigerator, for up to 6 weeks.

Clotted Cream

Eishta

Makes about 1 cup

950 ml (2 pt) full-cream milk
300 ml (10 fl oz) double cream

Pour the milk and cream into a wide heavy-based saucepan or deep frying pan. Place over low–medium heat and slowly bring to the boil, then reduce heat and simmer very gently for 1–1½ hours, until reduced to about 1 cup and thickened.

Transfer to a glass or ceramic bowl, cover with a clean tea towel and leave at room temperature for a few hours or overnight, to thicken. Refrigerate overnight before using (a thick crust will have formed).

Serve with pastries and desserts.

ꙮ Traditionally eishta was made with buffalo's milk, but full-cream cow's milk is a perfectly good substitute. The customary way of serving the cream is to roll it into a cylinder and slice into rounds 2.5 cm (1 in) thick.

Yoghurt, Lemon & Mint Sauce

Makes 1 cup

**1 clove garlic, crushed with
½ teaspoon salt**

**2 tablespoons (40 ml/1½ fl oz)
extra-virgin olive oil**

**3 tablespoons (60 ml/2 fl oz)
freshly squeezed lemon juice**

**⅔ cup (160 ml/6 fl oz) Greek-
style yoghurt**

freshly ground black pepper

1 teaspoon dried mint

Using a stick blender or food processor, blend all the ingredients together until well mixed. Adjust seasoning with extra lemon juice, salt or pepper according to taste.

🔊 When using dried mint, rub it between your fingers to crush it to a fine powder.

🔊 To make a yoghurt and garlic sauce, crush 1 clove garlic with a pinch of salt, then stir into 1 cup (250 ml/8½ fl oz) yoghurt. Serve with kebabs, or as a dip.

Special Ingredients

BURGHUL (also known as bulgar, bulgur and cracked wheat) The ground inner bran of the wheat grain. It is similar to couscous, but has a harder nutty texture. There are fine and coarse varieties available.

DUKKAH An Egyptian favourite, dukkah is a crushed dry mixture of nuts, seeds and spices, usually served with bread and olive oil. There are as many variations as there are family kitchens.

FETTA CHEESE A firm salty cheese, traditionally made from sheep or goat's milk. It is sold packed in brine.

FILO PASTRY Paper-thin sheets of pastry, used to make flaky pies and pastries. Usually multiple sheets are layered on top of each other, each brushed with butter. You have to work quickly with this pastry, as it quickly dries out – cover unused portions with cling wrap or a clean damp cloth. It is sold ready-rolled, either fresh or frozen.

HALOUMI CHEESE A firm, salty cheese, traditionally made with a mixture of sheep and goat's milk. It is suitable for grilling or frying due to its high melting point.

KASSERI CHEESE A soft-textured, pale-yellow cheese with a salty flavour. Traditionally made with unpasteurised sheep's milk, sometimes mixed with a little goat's milk.

KATAIFI PASTRY (konafa pastry) This finely shredded **filo** dough can be used for sweet or savoury dishes. As with filo sheets, cover unused portions with cling wrap or a damp cloth while you work, to stop it drying out. Kataifi is available from the freezer section of Middle Eastern and Greek food stores.

LOOMI (noomi) Dried, blackened lime. It is used as a seasoning throughout the Gulf region, either in powder form or as a whole dried fruit.

MOGHRABIEH A large couscous made from semolina. It is available from Middle Eastern food stores.

MORELLO CHERRIES Sour dark cherries often used in cooking.

OKRA Mild-flavoured, slender green vegetable seed pods. When cooked, they release a thick substance that acts as a thickening agent.

ORANGE-BLOSSOM WATER (orange-flower water) A solution of orange blossom oil in water. Used mainly as a flavouring in desserts.

POMEGRANATE MOLASSES A thick, dark, slightly tangy syrup made from pomegranates.

POMEGRANATE SEEDS The bright-red, sweet–tangy seeds of the pomegranate fruit. Use fresh when in season, or replace with dried cranberries.

PURSLANE An annual succulent commonly known in Australia as pigweed. The leaves, which have a sharp and slightly salty taste, have been used since ancient times in the Mediterranean region.

ROSEWATER A scented water made with rose petals, used to add a distinctive aroma and flavour to food, especially sweets.

SAMNEH (samna) A clarified butter that has a distinctive rich, nutty flavour and that does not burn when used at high temperatures. To make samneh, melt unsalted butter in a saucepan over low heat until it bubbles, then skim off any froth. Pour the clear yellow liquid through a muslin-lined sieve into a jar, leaving the milk solids in the saucepan. Store in a sealed jar in the refrigerator until required (it will keep for 6 months).

SUMAC A spice derived from the dried red-brown berries of the sumac plant. Usually bought in powdered form, it has a tangy flavour and can be substituted with lemon. Store in an airtight container in a cool dark place.

TAHINI A smooth, oily paste made from crushed sesame seeds and used as a base for Arabic dips and sauces. Available from supermarkets, health-food stores and Middle Eastern grocers. To make **tahini sauce**, thin tahini with a little water. Adding lemon juice will thicken the consistency.

TAMARIND PULP The sweet–tart pulp of the tamarind fruit. Available from Asian and Middle Eastern food stores, or from the Asian section of good supermarkets. Lemon juice can be used as an alternative.

VINE LEAVES Leaves of the grape vine, used for wrapping ingredients before cooking. Fresh or brined leaves may be used – if using brined leaves, you'll need to rinse them, then soak them in fresh water for about 20 minutes before use.

YOGHURT Yoghurt (usually Greek-style) is a common ingredient in Middle Eastern cooking. Often it is drained before use (see **drained yoghurt** on page 9). Cow's milk yoghurt must be stabilised before use to prevent it from curdling during lengthy cooking (see **stabilised yoghurt** on page 9).

Conversions

(Note: all conversions are approximate)

Important note: All cup and spoon measures given in this book are based on Australian standards. The most important thing to remember is that an Australian cup = 250 ml, while an American cup = 237 ml and a British cup = 284 ml. Also, an Australian tablespoon is equivalent to 4 teaspoons, not 3 teaspoons as in the United States and Britain. US equivalents have been provided throughout for all liquid cup/spoon measures. Equivalents for dry ingredients measured in cups/spoons have been included for flour, sugar and rising agents such as baking powder. For other dry ingredients (chopped vegetables, nuts, etc.), American cooks should be generous with their cup measures – slight variations in quantities of such ingredients are unlikely to affect results.

VOLUME

Australian cups/spoons	Millilitres	US fluid ounces
*1 teaspoon	5 ml	
1 tablespoon (4 teaspoons)	20 ml	¾ fl oz
1½ tablespoons	30 ml	1 fl oz
2 tablespoons	40 ml	1½ fl oz
¼ cup	60 ml	2 fl oz
⅓ cup	80 ml	3 fl oz
½ cup	125 ml	4 fl oz
¾ cup	180 ml	6 fl oz
1 cup	250 ml	8½ fl oz
4 cups	1 L	34 fl oz

*the volume of a teaspoon is the same around the world

>

SIZE

Centimetres	Inches
1 cm	³⁄₈ in
2 cm	¾ in
2.5 cm	1 in
5 cm	2 in
10 cm	4 in
15 cm	6 in
20 cm	8 in
30 cm	12 in

TEMPERATURE

Celsius	Fahrenheit
150°C	300°F
160°C	320°F
170°C	340°F
180°C	360°F
190°C	375°F
200°C	390°F
210°C	410°F
220°C	420°F

WEIGHT

Grams	Ounces
15 g	½ oz
30 g	1 oz
60 g	2 oz
85 g	3 oz
110 g	4 oz
140 g	5 oz
170 g	6 oz
200 g	7 oz
225 g	8 oz (½ lb)
450 g	16 oz (1 lb)
500 g	1 lb 2 oz
900 g	2 lb
1 kg	2 lb 3 oz

Index

LONDON, NEW YORK, MUNICH,
MELBOURNE AND DELHI

First published in Great Britain in 2011 by
Dorling Kindersley, 80 Strand, London, WC2R 0RL

A Penguin Company

Published by Penguin Group (Australia), 2010
250 Camberwell Road, Camberwell, Victoria 3124, Australia
(a division of Pearson Australia Group Pty Ltd)

10 9 8 7 6 5 4 3 2 1

Cover design by Marley Flory © Penguin Group (Australia)
Text design by Claire Tice and Marley Flory © Penguin Group (Australia)
Photography by Julie Renouf
Food styling by Lee Blaylock
Typeset in Nimbus Sans Novus by Post Pre-press Group, Brisbane, Queensland
Scanning and separations by Splitting Image P/L, Clayton, Victoria
Printed and bound in China by Everbest Printing Co. Ltd

A CIP catalogue record for this book is available from the British Library.

ISBN: 978-1-4053-6417-1

Discover more at www.dk.com